Praise for
GONE

'An engaging and entertaining
what we've lost and wha
Stephen Rutt, author of *The Seafarers* and *Wintering*

'Really, really well-written'
Chris Packham

'Michael Blencowe is an excellent story-teller. Each chapter is a good
read and the author unearths interesting information about the species,
the places where they live and the characters involved in trying to
conserve them or propelling them into the abyss of extinction.'
Mark Avery

'Quirky but compelling'
Stephen Moss

'A real feast…This is one of the saddest books you will ever read
and also, perversely, one of the most entertaining. … [Blencowe]
writes with such bubbling enthusiasm and a winning lightness
of touch that his book never becomes depressing.'
Marcus Berkmann, *Daily Mail*

'A lovely book. Personal and personable, Michael Blencowe shares his love
of recently extinct species by "meeting" their remains in the museums of
the world. He is an excellent guide to the recently lost and his passion for
spectacled cormorants, dodos, hula, moa and the rest positively shines through.'
Ross Barnett, author of *The Missing Lynx*

'Incredibly well-researched…a revelation of man's
effect on wildlife…A very good read.'
Wildlife Matters

'A very enjoyable book…As well as paying his respects to these
lost creatures, Blencowe also describes their tragic histories,
how they were discovered, and what became of them.'
Friends of Darwin Newsletter

'A fascinating, beautifully written book full of curious
and personal reflections on extinct creatures.'
Errol Fuller

To Tootles, my tortoise
Long May You Run

First published in 2021 by Leaping Hare Press,
an imprint of The Quarto Group.
The Old Brewery, 6 Blundell Street
London, N7 9BH,
United Kingdom

T (0)20 7700 6700
This paperback edition first published in 2022 by Aurum
www.QuartoKnows.com

A catalogue record for this book is available from the British Library.

ISBN 978-0-7112-7692-5
E-book ISBN 978-0-7112-5676-7
Audiobook ISBN 978-0-7112-6670-4

10 9 8 7 6 5 4 3 2 1

Typeset in Bembo by Claire Cater

Printed by CPI Group (UK) Ltd, Croydon, CR0 4YY

GONE

Michael Blencowe

Aurum

CONTENTS

The Booth Museum of Natural History

Three minutes to twelve. It's always three minutes to twelve.

I've tried to stay hopeful, I really have, but I've just never been able to shake the feeling that I'm constantly living in the last moments of a countdown. My entire life I've been shackled to the irrational belief that, at any second, the final whistle's going to blow and my life will come crashing down around me. So, I've always steered clear of long-term plans and avoided putting things off until tomorrow, just in case.

Switching on the news these days, my anxious foreboding seems less like a crazed state of mind and more like a reasonable response to the times we're living in. When I was a child, I imagined the world to be vast, balanced and indestructible, but sat here watching forests burn and icecaps melt it seems vulnerable, fragile and somehow smaller.

If other people can see hope for the future, I'm afraid I don't share their optimism. In fact, these days I'm finding myself increasingly adrift, disconnected from the other 7.8 billion *Homo sapiens* on the planet. I've started wondering whether I could defect from the human race altogether, maybe align myself with another species, one that doesn't seem hellbent on destroying the world. Aardvarks perhaps. They seem happy enough hiding away in a burrow all day, sneaking out at night to eat ants and cucumbers.

On those days when everything feels particularly hopeless, I always seem to find myself stood here, staring up at the weathered redbrick facade of this Victorian building. Set high above its embellished arches is a turquoise-rimmed clock. The time reads three minutes to twelve. It was three minutes to twelve when I first stood in this spot 30 years ago and, as far as anyone can recall, it has always been three minutes to twelve here. Not that I would want anybody to repair the rusted cogs and gears of that broken clock. Its motionless hands are just another of the many quirks that make this place so peculiar, so special, so timeless. For three decades this building has been my refuge against the world, and these days I need it more than ever. I step up through the bright red wooden doors and into the Booth Museum of Natural History. The world changes.

• • •

The Booth Museum exists in its own light, its own climate, its own time. I pause for a moment and close my eyes, soaking up the silence and allowing the world outside to fade away. Upon opening them I find the attendant at the front desk has lowered her paperback and is observing me suspiciously over the rim of her glasses. She nods a wary greeting, I respond with a smile and her thumb clicks the handheld tally counter adding me to today's total. Just another visitor at the Booth.

This extraordinary museum lurks unassumingly along Dyke Road, the tree-lined residential avenue that connects the coastal city of Brighton to one of England's best-loved landscapes: the rolling chalk hills of Sussex's South Downs. The museum was built in 1874 by ornithologist Edward Booth. Booth loved birds and he enthusiastically pursued his passion with his double-barrelled eight-bore percussion shotgun with dolphin hammers and Damascus steel barrels. A display cabinet holds Booth's gun along with the battered waterproof sandals and sou'wester he would pull on before tramping the wet marshes and moors hunting his quarry. His dream was to collect and display a specimen of every species of British bird in every plumage. There's a posed photograph of Booth – bearded, suited and steely-eyed – staring off camera as if he's just caught sight of some elusive warbler that requires shooting, stuffing and displaying in his collection.

Born in 1840, three years after Queen Victoria ascended the throne, Booth's behaviour, which today seems reprehensible, was typical of a nineteenth-century naturalist. Victorian society was enthralled by the natural world and they demonstrated their admiration through coveting, collecting and categorising it. Birds, butterflies, ferns, eggs, seaweeds, shells, you name it – if the Victorians could get their hands on it, they'd kill it, skin it, stuff it, press it and pin it. Their collections and curios, local or exotic, were displayed as a statement of their wealth, status and intellect. Just beyond the museum's entrance there's a reconstruction of a typical dimly lit parlour, the showcase of the Victorian home. Amid the shadows, the iridescent wings of tropical birds glimmer within glass domes and metallic blue butterflies lie meticulously ordered in serried ranks in the drawers of polished mahogany cabinets. Collecting turned into an obsession for certain men with the time, money and means: country clergy, colonels recently retired from the Empire's front lines or, in the case of Edward Booth, those who had inherited a substantial family fortune. When Booth's expanding bird collection threatened to engulf the family home, he built this museum to house his overflowing hobby. Yet, while other Victorian museums crammed their cabinets with regimented rows of birds in strict scientific order, Booth was a pioneer in presenting his specimens posed within three-dimensional replicas of their natural habitats: dioramas. A yellowhammer broadcasts a silent song from a facsimile of a farmyard fence. Guillemots and razorbills jostle on sculpted sea cliffs. Two swooping skylarks defend their nest from a predatory stoat. Inside each diorama a different species is immortalised in a frozen moment, a recreation of the life that Booth had taken away. Upon his own death in 1890, Booth bequeathed his museum to the people of Brighton.

● ● ●

A thousand glass eyes watch me as I wander along the galleries. Booth's dioramas are stacked from floor to ceiling, a wall of windows towering above me on either side of the aisle, each one offering a captivating glimpse into the private life of a British bird. Today, the museum holds much more than Booth's birds. Over time, as other local museums closed, the Booth opened its doors to their orphaned exhibits while also becoming the repository for the mahogany cabinets of those deceased clergymen, colonels and collectors. The museum slowly absorbed and amassed an incredible wealth of almost 1 million natural history specimens, everything from microscope slides of bacteria to mounted mammals – anthrax to zebras. Today, the Booth remains a special place for everyone from dinosaur-obsessed children to scientific researchers to people like me who value the inspiration, information and escape that this wonderful museum provides.

There are a million stories waiting to be told here. One of my favourite exhibits looms, threatening and fearsome, above the cuddly trilobites and David Attenborough activity books in the gift shop. This ridiculously large pair of palmate antlers – 2.75 metres (9 feet) across – once belonged to the world's mightiest deer, the Irish elk, which became extinct around 7,500 years ago. When impressive antlers such as these were first pulled, perfectly preserved, from Ireland's peat bogs, people were understandably confused as to why nobody had ever seen their owner alive. In 1697, after examining some antlers dug up near Dublin, Irish physician Dr Thomas Molyneux assured everyone that, while this colossal deer may no longer be found in Ireland, it would still exist in 'some other part of the world'. A suitably vague and reasonable explanation. After all, it was a great big world and there were still vast unexplored areas where a deer with ridiculous antlers could be hiding. Probably. And besides, Molyneux added, 'No real species of living creature is so utterly extinct as to be lost entirely out of this world.'

For most of human history, extinction was not a conceivable option. The prevailing belief was that God had created this perfect world and everything living in it in six days. The suggestion that some of His creations had malfunctioned and died out was not just controversial, it was blasphemous. It implied that God was fallible, that He had rushed Creation, cut a few corners, made some . . . mistakes.

In the Booth's 'hands-on' interactive gallery, two young boys in matching *Jurassic Park* T-shirts are running their tiny fingers over the ridges of an enormous tooth – the monstrous molar of an Indian elephant.

French naturalist Georges Cuvier spent an entire year running his fingers over elephants' teeth, studying every cusp and crown. He had arrived in Paris in the spring of 1795, just 17 months after Marie Antoinette had been executed at the guillotine. Although the worst terrors of the French Revolution had passed, Cuvier was ready to start a revolution of his own and, while nobody would lose their heads, he was about to blow everybody's minds. Cuvier was an astounding anatomist who, at the age of 26, was swiftly gaining his reputation as the 'pope of bones'. Toss him a tooth or pass him a piece of a pelvis and he could mentally reconstruct an entire animal. And so, on 4 April 1796, Cuvier took to the stage to deliver his first public lecture in Paris. For his first trick Cuvier split the elephant. Through comparing their dental structure Cuvier was the first person to identify that the elephants of India and Africa were in fact two distinctly separate species. Impressive. But Cuvier didn't stop there.

The two boys in front of me turn their hands to a second similarly massive tooth, which, according to the label, had been excavated from the chalk rocks on Brighton seafront and could be 200,000 years old. They excitedly flip a panel to discover which creature is missing this tooth, revealing a picture of something whopping, weird and . . . woolly.

Back in Paris in 1796, young Cuvier's lecture took an unexpected turn. He announced that during his anatomical investigations he had discovered another pair of pachyderms and introduced the world to the mammoth of Siberia and the mastodon of North America. His audience was no doubt stunned and probably still muttering 'Mon dieu!' to themselves, when Cuvier dropped his bombshell: mammoths and mastodons had existed, he said, in a 'world previous to ours', but now they were gone and never coming back. Cuvier had announced extinction. He had kicked open the door to a vanished world to reveal, in his words, 'a new highway to the genius who will dare to follow it'.

Not everyone was immediately eager to accept Cuvier's invitation to the land of the lost. The third president of the United States, Thomas Jefferson, wasn't sold on this new concept of extinction. In fact he believed that mastodons might still exist in the vast uncharted regions of the American West. He even instructed explorers Lewis and Clark to keep an eye out for anything big, hairy and tusky on their pioneering expedition to the Pacific in 1803, although in reality they were running about 10,000 years too late for such an encounter.

Meanwhile, Cuvier's discoveries didn't stop at mastodons and mammoths. Through further skeletal studies and his own excavations in Parisian quarries he continued to add more creatures to his menagerie of extinct animals: Irish elk, giant sloth, cave bear. Then, at the start of the nineteenth century, English fossil hunters Mary Anning, William Buckland and Gideon Mantell started unearthing the bones of monsters from beyond our wildest imaginations.

Gideon Mantell is a local hero with a whole display case dedicated to him at the Booth. A country doctor, Mantell was born, lived and worked in the nearby market town of Lewes, but his most celebrated discovery was made 18 kilometres (11 miles) north of the museum. Well, I say his discovery, but it is commonly believed that it was actually his wife Mary who, one morning in 1820 or 1821, noticed something unusual in a pile of rubble beside the road. That 'something unusual', a large brown tooth, would be one of history's most important discoveries. It would lead Gideon to seek, discover and describe the iguanodon and lead us all to the land of the dinosaurs.

● ● ●

Around another corner in the Booth I discover a new exhibit. A motley collection of bones, eggs and taxidermy animals stands on glass shelves in an illuminated cabinet. I recognise each exhibit immediately and a warm familiarity flows through me as if I've just opened up a box of old childhood toys. A stream of words that I haven't spoken in years spontaneously pours from my mouth like some whispered ancient incantation: 'moa, huia, thylacine, auk, aepyornis, conure, kōkako'. These relics represent creatures from all corners of the planet, species that have one tragic quality in common. Just like the Irish elk, the mammoth, the mastodon and the iguanodon, they are all extinct.

The last time I saw these extinct animals gathered together was in the pages of the books I'd read obsessively as a child. At school my friends idolised footballers; they wore their colours and filled sticker albums with their faces, but I couldn't think of anything more boring than football. I still can't. The team I supported were found in my books on extinction. I knew every detail of each animal's life and death. Entwined with each turbulent tale were stories of adventure: epic voyages of discovery with heroes, villains, mysterious islands and deep dark forests; stories that led me far, far away from my suburban cul-de-sac. I wanted to get closer to these creatures, visit their hallowed remains and explore the distant lands where they once lived. This collection of dead animals was strangely inspiring. There was something undeniably powerful about seeing my old team back together again: Extinction United. Yet they were missing their star player: the one extinct creature whose name is synonymous with death. I turn to discover it waiting for me on the other end of the gallery. Illuminated under spotlights stands a full-size replica skeleton along with a handful of authentic bones in the exclusive luxury of its own private display case. Well, it is the dodo. It's special.

• • •

That night I ventured into the dark corners of my loft and unearthed a box of books from my childhood, reacquainting myself with the animals from the Booth exhibit and other extinct creatures that also qualified for a place in their cabinet. Revisiting these familiar illustrations and images brought back memories of the days when my future felt like a blank page and my planet felt vast, unexplored and alive with possibilities. As a kid I even believed, like Dr Molyneux and President Jefferson, that there was still enough space for giant creatures to exist undetected. I remember sitting wide-eyed, watching a documentary about the yeti, that abominable snowman of the Himalayas, believing those distant mountains still held populations of ape-like creatures. As I grew older, the disenchanting touch of reason polluted my dreams. The deep dark forests and mysterious islands of my youth had all been explored and exploited. And with each passing year, the world that I had hoped I'd live in became smaller. Now it seemed with every news story another piece of my planet was disappearing.

I found myself escaping each week to a place where time stood still. Where it was always three minutes to twelve. Inside the Booth I'd stop and find some curious comfort from the cabinet of extinct species. What connection did I feel to these creatures? Did I belong in the cabinet with them? A relic of a bygone age, above a label which read 'A man out of time', 'A species on the verge of extinction'. No, it wasn't that. This collection of fur, skin, feathers and bones had reignited something in me, reminding me of the adventures I had promised myself as a boy. Stood here with these extinct animals it didn't feel like my time was running out. It began to feel like I was right back at the beginning.

CHAPTER ONE

Great Auk

Pinguinus impennis

GONE: December 1852

If I take one step forward it will be all over for me. Inches from my feet this rock ledge ends abruptly in a sheer drop, plunging down, down, down to where the sea surges and sighs far beneath me. The GPS that steered me here is flashing, advising me that my final destination awaits on the rocks 67 metres (220 feet) below. I ignore its suggestion and take a few steps back. A sudden gust of wind, straight in from the sea, rattles through the stapled papers I'm clutching: a fistful of photocopied maps, scribbled directions and a tenuous theory written by a good-looking dentist. On the top sheet, scrawled in pink fluorescent marker: 51.1781°N, 4.6673°W – the coordinates of this precise spot on our planet, a remote cliff edge on Lundy Island.

Lundy – a 5 kilometre/3 mile-long, flat-topped, steep-sided slab of granite – sits all alone in the middle of the Bristol Channel, the finger of water that separates Wales from England's tapering south-west peninsula. It's notorious for its history of piratical skulduggery and famous for its wildlife, especially the thousands of sea birds that return to nest on its cliffs each summer. A two-hour ferry ride connects Lundy to Devon, the county where I was born. Childhood Saturdays were spent with binoculars slung around my neck searching Devon's wild places for birds, each new discovery triumphantly crossed off 'The Checklist of the Birds of Devon' pinned alongside the *Star Wars* poster on my bedroom wall. On that list, sandwiched between terns and pigeons, were a group of streamlined sea birds: the auks. And among them, on that list of Devon's birds, were two words that blew my mind: great auk. The great auk wasn't to be found in my field guides to the birds of Britain, Europe or anywhere else for that matter.

It resided in my books on extinct animals: the last British bird to become globally extinct. But unlike other extinct animals from faraway places I could only dream of – New Zealand, the Galápagos, Mauritius – the great auk had once lived virtually on my doorstep here in Devon. It was wasn't just an extinct bird. It was my extinct bird.

The great auk's claim as a Devon resident was largely based on a story involving Lundy, a vicar and a large egg. In the February 1866 edition of the respected journal *The Zoologist*, the improbably named Reverend H.G. Heaven of Lundy told how he was once in possession of an 'enormous egg'. It was collected on Lundy by an islander who annually raided the eggs of the other auks: puffins, razorbills and guillemots (aka murres), which bred in their thousands along Lundy's cliffs. This man claimed the egg was from a pair of much larger birds, which the islanders named 'King and Queen Murr' because 'they were so big and stood up so bold like'. They never flew, just stayed near the water's edge and 'scuttled into it fast' if approached. They didn't nest on the cliffs like other auks but laid their egg 'a little way above high water'. Despite recently finding this egg, the islander reported that the King and Queen Murr had not been seen on Lundy since the early 1820s. The egg was eventually broken, the evidence lost. But the legend endured.

If you're unfamiliar with the great auk, the simplest way to describe it is 'it looks like a penguin'. Flightless, upright, waddling, black and white, it ticks all the boxes. But it's not that simple. Great auks don't look like penguins. Penguins look like great auks. The great auk was originally known by many names, one of which was 'penguin'. This may have come from the Welsh (or Cornish or Breton) *pen* (meaning 'head') and *gwyn* (meaning 'white') after the prominent white patch between the bird's eye and beak. Or simply from the Latin *pinguis* meaning 'fat and stupid', two insults that were levelled at the bird. When North Atlantic sailors eventually ventured to the southern hemisphere, they found similar black-and-white birds and called them all penguins too and the name stuck.

The southern penguins are unrelated to auks, which are represented by 24 species from the planet's cold northern seas. If you gathered all the auk species together for a family photo, the great auk would have towered freakishly over them all, a Gulliver among Lilliputians. At 75 centimetres (30 inches) tall and weighing up to 5 kilograms (11 pounds), the great auk looks like a razorbill that's been zapped with radiation and mutated to seven times its normal size. To the great auk, this monstrous mass was simple physics. The bigger you are, the better you sink; their bulky bodies allowed the birds to dive deeper and fish for longer. And if all you eat is fish, what's the point of flying anyway? The auk surrendered the power of flight but retained tiny, muscular wings to propel its streamlined body powerfully through the water. And then there's that beak, that impressive chunky, grooved beak. This mighty weapon, perfect for seizing and slicing fish, was celebrated in the auk's old name 'garefowl', one of many derivations of the Old Norse 'geirfugl' meaning 'spear bill'.

The great auk had evolved to be a master of the water. But there was one small imperfection: it had to lay an egg, and you can't lay an egg in the sea. For two months each summer, the great auk needed a solid surface and for that it had to venture to somewhere extremely dangerous – the land. The birds sought out the safety of remote islands where sloping shorelines allowed them access. But once ashore, the adaptations which had made the great auk the perfect underwater hunter left it totally vulnerable when it came face to face with the most vicious killer of them all.

● ● ●

When I was nine my dad took me on a day trip to Lundy Island. I spent the day watching thousands of guillemots and razorbills stacked on the sheer cliffs and I saw my first puffins – short, stocky sentries standing guard over their burrows in the turf. All day I dreamt of finding the place where my great auk once stood. As I grew older, I began to doubt Reverend Heaven's tale. The great auks of Lundy, like Father Christmas and the yeti, faded into childhood fantasies. Then, in the 1990s, a long-lost map of Lundy from 1822 was rediscovered, which added another element to Reverend Heaven's story. Tony Langham, a dentist from Surrey and an expert on Lundy's wildlife and history, studied the map and noticed a rock off Lundy's north-west coast labelled 'Bird Island'. Why, Tony asked, on an island swarming with sea birds, would one particular rock be named Bird Island? Cross-referencing the 1822 map with the reverend's tale of the King and Queen Murr's visit to Lundy in the early 1820s, Tony came to one conclusion: Bird Island must have been home to some special birds – great auks. Tony died shortly after his theory was published. His obituary praised his knowledge and love of Lundy as well as his 'film-star good looks'. His claim may be questionable, but if you can't put your faith in a handsome dentist who can you trust? Tony's remote rock was the link from my childhood home to the world of extinct animals. And now, 40 years later, I'm returning to Lundy, setting sail, along with a ferry full of other day-trippers, in search of Bird Island.

So that brings me here, my precarious cliff edge on Lundy. To find my page in the story of the great auk I need to get my bearings. I enter new coordinates – 49.7569°N, 53.1811°W – into the GPS and raise the device at arm's length above my head, those extra few inches vital for connecting to the satellites orbiting 19,000 kilometres (12,000 miles) above me. The digital compass swings to a new location almost exactly due west. I align myself and face the 3,373 kilometres (2,096 miles) of North Atlantic nothingness that stretch between Lundy and another remote granite rock rising from the sea off the coast of Newfoundland.

● ● ●

In May 1497, Italian navigator John Cabot would have passed Lundy as he sailed along the Bristol Channel. He too would have been clutching a compass and thinking about the thousands of miles of tempestuous ocean that lie due west. Under commission from King Henry VII of England, Cabot was in search of a north-west passage, a short cut to the riches of Asia. Perhaps King Henry's instructions were lost in translation because, instead of returning from his expedition laden with gold, he returned laden with cod. The king wasn't too impressed but others were very excited to hear Cabot's stories of a 'New Found

Land', where the surrounding seas were so thick with fish it would slow down a ship's progress. Soon hundreds of fishing boats from France, Portugal, Spain and England were risking the Atlantic journey to claim their share of the riches from the great cod fisheries of the Grand Banks of Newfoundland. Around 1501, a new island appeared on seafarers' navigational charts of the Grand Banks. At first it was named 'Isle of Birds', because this small barren island, just half a mile long by quarter of a mile wide, was covered with gannets and auks. Later it was known as 'Penguin Island' after the immense great auk colony there. But the name that eventually stuck was a reference to an even more memorable feature – it stank. Topped with a deep, foul-smelling crust of guano, bird droppings deposited by millions of sea birds over generations, it was named Funk Island.

French explorer Jacques Cartier, also seeking that fabled north-west passage, visited Funk Island in 1534 and described the island as containing birds 'whose numbers are so great as to be incredible', detailing the breeding gannets, guillemots and 'exceedingly fat' great auks. By the 1500s, the world population of the great auk was almost entirely restricted to the north-west Atlantic. There were other scattered 'Penguin Islands' where dwindling populations of the bird nested each summer, but Funk was the auk's stronghold; the colony here has been estimated at 100,000 birds. Funk Island would be the first island many European ships would encounter after months at sea – a welcome, if somewhat stinky, navigational marker. For hungry sailors it was also a filling station stocked with fat, flightless birds that were easy to catch. Men stuffed their bellies then stuffed their barrels with salted auk for the onward journey. Legends tell of auks herded by the hundred along gangplanks and into boats. The annual great auk banquet took its toll on the colony, but worse was to come. The bird's soft, silky feathers were in demand to stuff quilts, mattresses and pillows. Men moved onto Funk Island each summer, setting up camps so the great auk harvest could be undertaken on an industrial scale. Auks were corralled into stone pens to await their deaths. Cauldrons were hung over fires, the birds boiled alive to loosen their feathers then plucked and slung back on the fires still alive, their body fat fuel for the flames. The slaughter was callous, barbaric and relentless, an auk apocalypse. By 1800, the bonfires of Funk Island stopped burning. The great auk was extinct in North America.

Across the North Atlantic the great auk still clung to a perilous existence, with the world population now largely confined to one Icelandic island. There were other auks too, castaways seemingly adrift from the colony, which attempted to breed on the rocky shores of Britain's remote islands. But nowhere was safe. A pair of auks on the Orkney Islands were stoned and shot in 1812. On the remote Scottish island of St Kilda a lone great auk was captured in 1821, but, when its cries seemingly conjured up a storm, it was declared to be a witch and beaten to death. Maybe around this time a pair of great auk tried to find some sanctuary on Lundy. The last British great auk was captured 200 kilometres (125 miles) from Lundy near Waterford, south-west Ireland, in 1834.

I'm not comfortable with heights, but I cautiously edge my way forward. Peering down over the cliff edge, there is Bird Island. 'Island' is overstating it. It's a vaguely pyramidal rock, barely separated from Lundy. Its sea-scoured lower shelves slope gradually into the sea, contrasting with a tower of darker rock that rises above the high-water mark. Here a tight cluster of razorbills huddle on a summit splattered white with guano. The feeling of accomplishment at locating this remote rock is overtaken by a sudden realisation. Bird Island is the perfect home for a great auk. The surge of the sea through the gully would deliver an auk on to its shallow sloping rocks. From there it would be an easy waddle to where its enormous lone egg could be safely laid above the high tide. The great auk *was* here. The vicar, the egg, the good-looking dentist. It was all true. In my mind I can see them. The King and Queen Murr, standing at the sea's edge, their heads held high.

In 1830 just one great auk colony remained, in the cold waters 40 kilometres (25 miles) off southern Iceland. Here the birds gathered and nested each summer on the Geirfuglasker, an isolated island defended by deadly currents and ominous superstitions. Only the bravest men dared venture here and in some years no men landed here at all. The birds had found their fortress; maybe here, out of reach on the Geirfuglasker, they could rebuild their numbers. Then, in March 1830, the island sank. The Geirfuglasker was part of a chain of volcanic islands and, during a series of explosive eruptions, it disappeared dramatically beneath the waves. With islands and options vanishing before their eyes, these last refugee auks had one final hope: Eldey, a sloping chunk of volcanic rock just 200 metres (650 feet) long, 75 metres (250 feet) high and a lot closer to Iceland. It was here they would make their final stand. But the auk was now wanted not for food or feathers but as a museum exhibit.

As naturalists and collectors realised the rarity of the great auk, museums worldwide scrambled to secure specimens. High prices were offered to the men who could help them complete their collections. I programme the last set of coordinates into my GPS – 63.7408°N, 22.9580°W – and turn north-west to where Eldey lies in the cold Icelandic waters 1,760 kilometres (1,094 miles) away from Lundy. According to the story, it happened exactly 175 years ago today.

●　●　●

On the evening of 2 June 1844, eight oars propelled 14 men from the sheltered bay of Kyrkjuvogr on Iceland's south-west coast. By morning they had reached Eldey. The world's last known pair of great auks watched as they approached. With the weather deteriorating, landing men on Eldey was going to be dangerous, but not impossible. Three men, Brandsson, Iselfsson and Ketilsson, scrambled onto the treacherous rock, instantly spotted their quarry and started scaling the sloping ledge. Brandsson went after the closest bird. It was quickly cornered and caught. The second bird was running. Ketilsson lost his nerve but Iselfsson hauled himself up. Guillemots and razorbills cackled and scattered, taking flight as the great auk fled along a precarious ledge that rose to a sheer drop. Just ahead, the freedom of the open sea beckoned, but something was holding the bird back. Iselfsson's strong hands closed around the auk's neck. There was no struggle, no sound, just a sigh and the auk's eyes closed forever. The two strangled birds were slung on board. The wind was rising, the breakers were crashing against Eldey –

it was 'Satan's weather', the men said. The boat cleared the surging waves, the sea calmed, the men rowed home. Back on the mainland, money changed hands. The birds were sold, skinned and shipped to a dealer in Denmark. Ketilsson would later tell that he had found an egg that day but it had been cracked. And so it was left there, the life leaking from it, on a lava slab on Eldey.

The Natural History Museum of Denmark holds 14 million objects in its collections and a new exhibition 'Precious Things' showcases 78 of their most beautiful and valuable treasures. In the gift shop I buy my ticket and guidebook. As I try to decipher Danish, I pass a 17-metre (56-foot) diplodocus and some of Charles Darwin's barnacles, then enter a low-lit maze of corridors containing skeletons, artwork and Hans Christian Andersen's snail collection. I'm in search of exhibit Number 49. Inside a small, darkened room with the sanctity of a shrine, I find an altar-like shelf upon which, in a halo of soft light, sit four glass apothecary jars. In the right-hand jar, preserved in an amber fluid, are the eyes of the last pair of great auk killed on Eldey, the same eyes that saw the boat, and extinction, approaching in 1844. The jar to the left contains their two perfect hearts. It's hard not to imagine those final, panicked, pulsing beats 175 years ago as their species died out forever. The last great auks – preserved forever in legend and in 70 per cent ethanol in a glass jar on a shelf in Copenhagen. Standing in front of them, head held high, is a great auk. There are around 80 taxidermy specimens of the great auk in the world's museums and collections, almost all of them taken from Eldey between 1830 and 1844.

Peter Hosner, the museum's assistant professor and curator of birds, pulls open the doors of a large metal cabinet. The bottom shelf is home to the most impressive set of great auk remains on the planet. There are skulls and bones from Funk Island and jars containing the remaining viscera of the Eldey auks: liver, ovaries, intestines, lungs, trachea and syrinx, the bird's vocal organs, all of which, Peter says, were originally removed and thrown into a barrel of brandy. At the front of the cabinet is one of the museum's prized possessions: a great auk in white-throated winter plumage, a rarity as almost all other specimens were collected when the birds came ashore to breed in their smart summer attire. Peter points out its frayed wing feathers, which have given rise to the claim that this bird was caged alive for a period. Strangely, neither of the museum's taxidermy specimens are the birds captured on Eldey in 1844. Although they left their hearts (and other organs) in Copenhagen, the skins of the Eldey auks were sent elsewhere, their whereabouts unknown.

In 2017, during her PhD, Jessica Thomas, a student at Bangor University in Wales and the University of Copenhagen, working with a team of researchers, investigated the mystery of the missing auks. By taking ancient DNA samples from the auk organs in Copenhagen, Jessica was able to compare them with samples from five other auk museum specimens suspected to be the Eldey birds. The male Eldey great auk was tracked down to a taxidermy bird on display in the Royal Belgian Institute of Natural Sciences in Brussels. The final resting place of the female Eldey auk remains unknown – although a specimen held in the Cincinnati Museum of Natural History & Science seems a possible candidate.

Jessica also laid another mystery to rest. After the auk vanished, many people would not accept that we were the sole reason for the bird's extinction. There must have been other environmental factors at play that pushed the bird over the brink. Using ancient DNA taken from the bones of 41 different great auks ranging from 15,000 years old to the last two Eldey individuals, Jessica and her colleagues were able to investigate and compare the birds' genetic diversity. A low genetic diversity would leave the species vulnerable to environmental changes, with the entire population being less able to adapt and recover. However, the samples showed high genetic diversity. There was no evidence that populations were already declining or at risk of extinction prior to the intensive slaughter. They were doing just fine until we turned up. Amid Jessica's statistical models and dense calculations is the scientific evidence that proves man can be brutal and thoughtless. We wiped this unique species off the planet in a few short centuries, denying me and millions of others the thrill of living alongside this incredible animal.

• • •

While the Eldey auks may have been the last known breeding pair, the last sighting is now considered to be from December 1852, when Colonel Henry Drummond-Hay, the first president of the British Ornithologist's Union, sailing on a steamer over the Grand Banks of Newfoundland, observed a bird swimming alongside the boat and had 'no doubt in his mind' what he saw. It dived beneath the waves and the great auk, the giant flightless sea bird of the northern hemisphere, disappeared forever.

The ferry from Lundy moors at the harbour in Bideford, the day-trippers disperse and I stroll back to the car park passing a statue of the author and naturalist Charles Kingsley. A temporary sign informs me that next week is his 200th birthday. Kingsley's hugely popular fantasy book *The Water Babies,* published in 1863, featured the last great auk, the 'Gairfowl', stood on the Allalonestone. The Gairfowl told her sad tale of vanishing volcanic islands and a once great nation of birds slaughtered, beaten, shot and eaten. 'This was the Gairfowl's story', wrote Kingsley, 'and, strange as it may seem, it is every word of it true.' The last great auk stands all alone, crying tears of pure oil. 'And soon I shall be gone, my little dear', she says, 'and nobody will miss me.'

She was wrong.

CHAPTER TWO

Spectacled Cormorant

Phalacrocorax perspicillatus

GONE: *c.* 1852

I've always thought of cormorants as cantankerous, cranky old grouches. There's something vaguely unsettling, even slightly sinister, about these reptilian, long-necked birds cloaked in glossy black feathers. Wary and constantly vigilant, they always look like they're up to no good. For me, cormorants are birds of Wednesday evening. It's then that I always see them, gathered on one particular electricity pylon by the estuary, an ominous portent as I drive to my local supermarket on the joyless weekly shopping trip. A dozen black silhouettes, wings spread wide, crucified against the clouds – a characteristic pose used to dry their damp feathers after their aquatic hunts. Cormorants are solitary fishermen but gather at dusk as if driven by the compulsion to share their tales of the day's catch, outstretched wings boasting of the one that got away.

If you've ever seen the sea you've seen a cormorant. The 40 or so members of the cormorant family (along with their allied species, the shags) are ubiquitous fixtures of the world's shorelines. They vary in size from the pygmy cormorant of south-east Europe and Asia (340 grams/12 ounces) to the flightless cormorant of the Galápagos Islands (around 3.5 kilograms/7½ pounds). But, 200 years ago, there was a cormorant that tipped the scales at over 6 kilograms (13¼ pounds), the spectacled cormorant. This 'King of the Cormorants' had only ever been encountered on one remote, inhospitable island shaped like a jagged dagger blade: Bering Island in the Bering Sea between Russia and North America.

In 1741, the first naturalist to visit Bering Island and set eyes on the spectacled cormorant was struck by the bulk of the bird, writing, 'In size and plumpness they exceed the allied species'. In his battered notebook he described the bird as 'a special kind of large sea raven with a callow white ring around the eyes and red skin about the beak'. Of its behaviour he noted, 'From the ring around the eyes and the clown-like twistings of the head and neck, it appears quite a ludicrous bird.' These meagre field notes would be the only observations written by someone who saw a spectacled cormorant alive. Less than a century after its discovery it was extinct, and only seven specimens of the bird now survive. Today, at one o'clock, I have an appointment to meet one.

● ● ●

The rural English market town of Tring, 48 kilometres (30 miles) north-west of central London, is home to 12,000 people and two spectacled cormorants. Above Tring Shoe Repairs on the narrow, bustling high street, a giant painted hand points: 'This way to the Zoological Museum'. Tring's natural history museum was the idea of a seven-year-old boy who, in 1875, announced, 'Mama, Papa. I am going to make a museum.' If it were my parents I'd have probably been supplied with a cardboard box, but then my parents were not part of a dynasty that had amassed the largest private fortune the world had ever seen. For his 21st birthday Walter Rothschild got his museum, built especially for him on the edge of the family's Tring estate, and he eagerly stocked it with the natural history specimens he had collected since childhood. Rothschild would become the eminent zoologist and collector of his day. From his Tring headquarters he sent forth his minions. Hundreds of hunters on Rothschild's payroll battled stormy seas, the beasts of the jungle, cannibals and exotic diseases as they scoured the globe for animals, which, alive or dead, were transported to Tring to fill Rothschild's museum. Each shipped specimen was carefully unpacked, named, classified, labelled and arranged in meticulous order. Rothschild soon possessed the greatest natural history collection amassed by one person: over 2 million pinned butterflies and moths, 300,000 bird skins, 200,000 birds' eggs; from fleas to elephants, aardvarks to zebras, great auks to thylacines. Rothschild was a big bear of a man, an eccentric character famously photographed riding around Tring Park on a giant tortoise or driving a carriage pulled by trained zebras through London to Buckingham Palace. He opened the doors of the Walter Rothschild Zoological Museum to the public in 1892 and after his death he donated his collection to the nation.

This incredible Victorian museum is now a satellite site of London's Natural History Museum, containing grandiose galleries of Rothschild's extraordinary specimens. My one o'clock appointment is in the rather less impressive office block shrouded in scaffolding around the corner. Despite its underwhelming exterior, the Natural History Museum at Tring's bird collection contains a wealth of treasures. Its cabinets and drawers hold 750,000 specimens representing 95 per cent of the world's bird species, which are available, upon request, for study by researchers and scientists. I'm no scientist, but I have kindly been granted an appointment and, in my welcoming conversation with senior curator Mark Adams, I seem to have both suitably impressed him with my spectacled cormorant knowledge and managed to contain my excitement. Since I was a boy I have obsessed over this extinct bird's details and history. As Mark fetches the cormorant, my fingers drum the tabletop in anxious anticipation. I take a deep breath to calm my nerves as I hear his returning footsteps on the storeroom floor.

● ● ●

When a spectacled cormorant is placed in front of me, my delirium dims. Up until now I have only seen illustrations of the bird in my books. In artists' imaginations it elegantly swam or perched proudly on some rocky shore, ludicrous and colourful. In front of me, lifeless and laid in the clinical surroundings of a white tray, the bird looks genuinely tragic, like some dejected clown. Those comical white rings around its eyes have yellowed with age, the once bright make-up around its beak now dry, cracked and colourless. 'You can pick it up if you like', Mark says. I wouldn't have dreamt of touching it, assuming such a precious specimen would be sacrosanct, but I reach forward and scoop my hands underneath its ancient body. I gently raise it towards me with wonder and affection, as if a midwife had just handed me my newborn child. Suddenly I'm struck by the realisation that I am, for the first time in my life, touching an extinct animal. I cradle its head to support its long, fragile neck, its hook-tipped beak now almost touching my nose. As I hold the bird closer to my chest, its feathers glitter purple and green under the museum lights and a warm petroleum iridescence flows over its body, an illusion of life. I can almost smell the Bering Sea in its feathers, can hear the bird's guttural gargles. With its head held high the spectacled cormorant looks altogether more dignified. I notice long, white, whiskery feathers flowing from its head, which, along with its spectacles, bestow an air of wisdom on the bird. It appears less clown-like now, more like some venerable Chinese philosopher. I picture it stood, wings outstretched, on some windswept rock, preaching its proverbs to any passing puffins that will listen.

A forced cough snaps me from my dreaming and I look up to see Mark staring at me with some concern as I sit cuddling his cormorant. He extracts the bird from my embrace, placing it back on the tray while I attempt to regain some scientific integrity by enquiring about the specimen's origin. Mark lifts one of the bird's ancient webbed feet and shows me the equally ancient label attached to it, bearing a name elegantly written in faded ink: Captain Belcher.

● ● ●

In September 1837, naval officer Edward Belcher was leading an expedition aboard HMS *Sulphur*, exploring and surveying the Pacific coast. After an evening admiring the aurora borealis, the *Sulphur* visited the settlement of Sitka on the shores of Alaska. Here they received a warm greeting from the Russian governor, Ivan Kupreanof. Belcher's expedition explored the area, meeting the native people of the region. On their final evening, the *Sulphur's* crew were thrown a party where Belcher waltzed the night away. The following morning, as HMS *Sulphur* sailed out of Sitka Sound, they carried on board a unique gift from the governor: a specimen of a spectacled cormorant. Kupreanof had been collecting examples of all the territory's wildlife and bestowed upon Captain Belcher a rare specimen of the giant cormorant of Bering Island. At the time little was known about the mysterious bird that sailed south on the *Sulphur.* Where exactly did it nest? Could it fly? Did it even still exist?

In 1882, desperate to answer these questions, a naturalist sailed north for Bering Island. Part of his mission was to discover whether the spectacled cormorant still survived and, if so, to make detailed observations. Like any great naturalist of his era, he carried with him the two qualities required for such an expedition: an enquiring mind and a big gun.

• • •

At noon on 5 April 1882, the steamer *Aleksander II* left San Francisco's Golden Gate and, dogged by strong westerly winds, made slow progress as it sailed north. On board was Dr Leonhard Stejneger. Stejneger was a passionate zoologist, herpetologist and ornithologist and an enthusiastic dancer. If there was music playing, Stejneger would be out of his seat and jigging 'cross the floor (this particular talent isn't relevant to our story, but I know I'd be particularly aggrieved if a biographer ever listed my achievements and my own unique dancefloor performances weren't commemorated). Twenty-five days after leaving San Francisco, Stejneger noted that the Bering Sea welcomed the *Aleksander II* with its customary greeting, 'a veritable hurricane from the east north-east'.

On Bering Island, Stejneger chartered a local boat and crew and circumnavigated the island. He endured dense fog and plagues of mosquitoes as he scanned the coast and cliffs for a giant cormorant with white rings around its eyes. At one point he capsized a sealskin kayak and, while slowly drowning, he became utterly entranced by the hypnotic movements of the light diffused through the water. His enjoyment and impending death were interrupted by his companions, who dragged him back onshore, where he was revived and regained consciousness. Stejneger interrogated every islander he met about the spectacled cormorant. Many recalled a time when the bird 'was plentiful on the rocks', especially on the outlying islet of Ariy Kamen, a 50 metre/164 foot-high chunk of granite famous for its seabird colonies. Could this small island have been the last refuge of the spectacled cormorant? Was it their equivalent of the great auk's Eldey? When Stejneger offered a 'very high reward' to any man who could help him locate the cormorant, the local people just laughed. The last spectacled cormorant was seen 'about 30 years ago' they said. This puts a rough date for the extinction of the bird at 1852, the same year that the last great auk disappeared under the waves. Stejneger was heavy-hearted. In his expedition report he wrote, 'you will not be more disappointed than I am in learning that there is no hope whatever in getting a specimen'. The 'King of the Cormorants' was gone.

• • •

Leonhard Stejneger had arrived 30 years too late to acquire his own spectacled specimen; however, he did not return from his cormorant quest empty-handed. While exploring the north-west coast of Bering Island, Stejneger scrambled up a steep escarpment and discovered a seam of animal bones buried in the sand and sod. He delicately unearthed a pelvis, which he identified as belonging to the spectacled cormorant. He started to dig and excavated 21 more bones. Back at the Smithsonian Institution in Washington these bones were meticulously measured, described and illustrated and gave us more insight into the living bird. Stejneger wrote: 'The spectacled cormorant appears to have been a much heavier bird than the great cormorant and a bird of weaker flight with more robust and muscular legs, and a more slender, feeble head and neck.' The bones indicated the wings had been disproportionately small; if this huge cormorant could fly it probably wasn't airborne for long. Leonhard Stejneger would rise to the esteemed role of head curator of biology at the Smithsonian Institution. You'd still find him out on the dancefloor at the age of 85 until, under the orders of his doctor, he hung up his dancing shoes. He died six years later in 1943 and always lamented that the spectacled cormorant, 'the largest and handsomest of its tribe', had been overlooked compared to the great auk, whose extinction had seemingly occurred simultaneously yet had attracted much scientific attention and regret. Leonhard Stejneger left behind a huge legacy of knowledge about the natural world. And he also left behind a drawer of cormorant bones at the Smithsonian Institution.

• • •

Stejneger's spectacled cormorant bones may not be as impressive as the seven shimmering skins secured by Governor Kupreanof, but in 2017 these bones would play a crucial role in our understanding of the spectacled cormorant's world.

A team from the National Museum of Nature and Science in Tokyo had undertaken palaeontological excavations in the coastal Shiriya region of north-east Japan in the 1960s and 1980s, unearthing bones dating from the late Pleistocene era around 129,000–11,700 years ago. Among their discoveries were the remnants of a large cormorant – larger than any of the four cormorant species that can be found in Japan today. In 2010, Junya Watanabe of Kyoto University was studying these bones and, at first, believed them to be from a new species of large cormorant. However, when he learnt of the extinct spectacled cormorant, Junya realised he needed to undertake some detective work. In 2014, he travelled to the Smithsonian Institution in Washington and, at a small wooden desk sandwiched between storage cabinets, he set out his notebook and calipers. Junya removed the Bering Island bones from their small cardboard containers and started taking precise measurements of femora, humeri, coracoids and pterygoids. They were an exact match to the bones discovered in Japan. 'Before our report, there was no evidence that the spectacled cormorant lived outside of Bering Island', said Watanabe. But here was proof that the spectacled cormorant once had a much wider distribution, which may have stretched 2,400 kilometres (1,500 miles) from Japan along the string of Kuril Islands to its last refuge on Bering Island. What could have caused its avian empire to crumble? Twenty thousand years ago, when the ice sheets of the north reached their greatest extent, plankton levels in the sea around Shiriya dropped drastically. This would have had a massive impact on marine food webs and ultimately seabird populations. The excavations in north-east Japan have also uncovered the bones of a flightless sea duck (*Shiriyanetta hasegawai*) and a large guillemot (*Uria onoi*). Both these species seem to have become extinct after the late Pleistocene, while the spectacled cormorant endured. However, by the start of the eighteenth century it had retreated to remote Bering Island – a final relic population. Yet here it seems that the spectacled cormorants had found their Shangri-La, a small corner of the globe where they could make their stand. So, what had gone wrong? Why had they disappeared?

The spectacled cormorants had certainly seemed to be thriving here once. Anyone landing on Bering Island at the start of the eighteenth century would have remarked on their abundance. But here lies the answer to our riddle, because at the start of the 1700s no one had landed on Bering Island. Ever. Bering Island didn't even have a name. It was just an undiscovered island hidden in a godforsaken corner of our planet. But all that was about to change. Hold on tight folks, it's going to be a rocky ride.

CHAPTER THREE

Steller's Sea Cow

Hydrodamalis gigas

GONE: *c.* 1768

Georg Wilhelm Stöller was born on 10 March 1709 and he died on 10 March 1709. The midwife, suitably satisfied that this was the end of the line for the stillborn Stöller, packed her bags and left. This chapter would be considerably shorter if it wasn't for a family friend who, through dogged determination and the application of hot blankets, managed to miraculously revive the little fellow. A hesitant start for a determined man.

I have to confess something here: I love this guy. After learning about his discoveries in my books of extinct animals and reading the journal of his epic adventures he became a hero to me. It's his attitude, humanity, enthusiasm – and maybe I see something of myself in him, too. As a child Stöller was, like me, obsessed with nature. He spent all his time in the flower-filled fields and oak forests around his home in Windsheim, Germany. And, like me, he dreamt of exploration, discovery and a wide world beyond his hometown. Unlike me, he actually did something about it.

At the age of 20, Stöller headed to the University of Wittenberg to study theology. His parents waved farewell, believing he'd return someday as a priest. They never saw him again. Two years later in 1731, while studying medicine, botany and zoological dissection at the University of Halle, Stöller made the bizarre claim that he had once meddled in the black arts and made a grim prophecy about his future: 'I will travel to the extreme end of Europe, suffer shipwreck, be cast upon an uninhabited island and die in a distant country far from here.'

● ● ●

At the start of the eighteenth century, there were still plenty of distant, undiscovered lands that could fulfil Stöller's prophecy. Siberia and the coastline of the North Pacific remained largely uncharted. In St Petersburg, the great Danish explorer Vitus Bering was preparing to lead the Second Kamchatka Expedition, a massively ambitious venture involving a cast of thousands. Bering's tasks included mapping the eastern extremities of Siberia and the western coast of North America and figuring out whether the two continents were actually joined. This expedition was the opportunity Stöller had dreamt of. At the age of 25, he left Germany and travelled to St Petersburg, arriving in November 1734, determined to make a name for himself. When he discovered the Russians didn't have an 'ö' in their alphabet, he did indeed make a name for himself: Steller. The rebranded Steller caught some lucky breaks; he met all the right people, ingratiated himself with the Russian Academy of Sciences and eagerly consumed information on Siberian and American wildlife in the Academy's vast library.

Steller's golden ticket eventually arrived when he was requested as a naturalist on the Second Kamchatka Expedition. He raced across the frozen wastes of Russia, snugly wrapped in furs in his horse-drawn troika, to catch up with Captain Commander Vitus Bering. He travelled for three years, crossed the Ural Mountains and traversed the wild, volcanic Kamchatka peninsula by dogsled where he spent time with the native Itelmen people, learning their customs and the medicinal powers of vitamin-rich berries and plants. After finally meeting Bering, Steller was offered a place aboard his ship, the *St Peter*. Steller's official title would be mineralogist, although Bering required Steller's skills as a doctor, naturalist and minister. On 4 June 1741, the *St Peter* and its companion ship the *St Paul* set sail from Avacha Bay in Kamchatka in search of America. The *St Peter* carried 78 men: officers, soldiers, grenadiers, gunners, sailors, shipbuilders and one excited scientist, Georg Wilhelm Steller. Things started going wrong from the very start – the *St Peter* and *St Paul* became separated and lost in the fog. Steller's observations of sea birds and seaweed indicated their proximity to land but his suggestions were ignored and ridiculed by the officers. Each evening he grumbled about them in his journal.

The crew of the *St Peter* finally sighted Alaska on 16 July (Steller had seen it the day before but no one had believed him). Steller was desperate to get ashore and explore this vast unknown wilderness fully. But, having found America, Bering immediately made plans to turn back home, his job done. Steller was furious; he had waited his whole life for this moment. At this point I half expected him to stick his notebook between his teeth and start swimming to Alaska. Next day Bering relented, allowing Steller a day ashore where, in a whirlwind of botanical recording, he described 144 plant species. Steller observed many unfamiliar birds and collected one specimen of a vivid blue crow, Steller's jay, one of three birds that bear his name. The following morning the *St Peter* weighed anchor and headed back to Kamchatka. Steller was still cursing, 'ten years the preparation for this great undertaking lasted, and ten hours were devoted to the work itself'.

From then on things really started going wrong. Horribly wrong. The crew succumbed to scurvy. Steller advised that everyone should follow the native Itelmen's example: drink fresh water and eat berries and herbs. But, out of spite more than anything, he was again ignored. With the crew dying, the ship sailed into a series of unimaginably ferocious storms. For months the *St Peter* was torn apart and tossed around the North Pacific like a piece of driftwood. Steller himself took the wheel while, to his horror, the superstitious sailors unceremoniously threw their comrades' corpses overboard to appease the storm. On 6 November 1741, after two months in this tempest, what's left of the *St Peter* and her crew were flung on to the rocks of a barren island.

The crew, believing that they were back on the Kamchatka peninsula, awaited their rescue, but a few days after the shipwreck Steller stood on the shore scratching his head, amazed and perplexed by the sight before him. In the shallow waters a huge creature lay half submerged in the water. Momentarily, its head rose from the water and it softly exhaled, blowing saltwater from its nostrils. There were dozens of these bizarre beasts snorting and sighing in the shallows all along the bay. Steller had no idea what these creatures were but he was certain of one thing – they were not in Kamchatka anymore. Wherever they were, they were on their own.

● ● ●

Steller cared and cooked for the scurvy-stricken crew the best he could. His journal entries read like a report direct from hell itself: disease, hunger, storms, thirst, lice, damp, cold, despair. 'Everywhere we looked on nothing but depressing and terrifying sights', he wrote. Men screamed in agony, unable to eat because their scurvy-stricken gums had 'swollen like a sponge, brown-black and grown high over the teeth and covering them'. On 8 December, the illustrious Bering himself died, 'more from hunger, cold, thirst, vermin and grief than from a disease'. The island would later be named in his honour. The Arctic foxes that swarmed around the camp, at first inquisitive and mischievous, were now a constant torture. They terrorised the men, stealing everything they could and attempting to eat the dying. While one man was urinating from his hut, a fox bit into his 'exposed part' and would not let go. It's right about now in the story that I'm happy I didn't leave home to become an explorer. Although surrounded by death, Steller remained healthy, as driven and inquisitive as ever. Between nursing the crew he still managed to nip off for some bird-watching. On his explorations he became the first man to discover the 'ludicrous' spectacled cormorant, a giant white sea eagle, a colourful sea duck and rookeries of hulking sea lions. He fastidiously detailed these discoveries in his notebooks. But one creature captivated him above all others.

Measuring up to 9 metres (30 feet) in length and weighing up to 10 tonnes, Steller's sea cow was a colossal marine mammal, longer than a killer whale and heavier than an elephant. Like the other animals on the island, the sea cows were unaccustomed to humans and so allowed Steller to crouch alongside, stroking them as they floated into the shallows on the high tide. Their thick skin was 'mangy, wrinkled, rough, hard and tough' and looked like 'the bark of an ancient oak', offering them protection against predators, rocks and icebergs. Their bodies were so bloated and buoyant that they couldn't submerge. Instead, they silently bobbed like giant corks in herds along the bay, grazing on the dense kelp forest, their heads almost constantly underwater, oblivious to danger. They had thick, bristly, flexible lips, and instead of teeth two bony plates would grind the thick seaweed like millstones. Every few minutes their noses would rise above water to draw breath. Aside from the occasional snort ('such as a horse makes in blowing his nose'), they quietly got on with the important business of floating and feeding. Their huge bodies tapered to a forked fluke tail, which slowly moved from side to side to propel the animal, although a heavy beat on the surface of the water would give the sea cow a burst of speed. When stuffed with seaweed they would swim further offshore, roll over onto their backs and snooze. Steller's notes on their courtship read like a romantic novel. The female would swim gently to and fro in the water with the male following her until 'as if tired and under compulsion she throws herself on her back'. The male would then take his opportunity and 20 tonnes of sea cow would 'rush into each other's embrace'.

Back in the camp, the surviving crew of the *St Peter*, under Steller's guidance, care and diet, slowly began to recover. Alongside fur seal and sea otter, spectacled cormorant was also on the menu. These clumsy birds were easily captured and were encased – feathers and all – in clay and roasted inside a heated pit, a cooking technique Steller had learnt in Kamchatka. The cormorants were plentiful and surprisingly tasty; 'the flesh of one could feed three starving men', wrote Steller.

When the skylark's song heralded the start of spring, the men's thoughts turned to escape. Their plan was to dismantle the remnants of the *St Peter* and build a much smaller vessel capable of carrying them home. After eating most of the local wildlife, searching for food further afield now took up valuable time, time that should be spent shipbuilding. The answer to their problems was floating right before their eyes but only now were the men strong enough to do something about it.

• • •

In May, the men's first attempt at hooking a sea cow from the shore resulted in both hook and rope being dragged out to sea by the powerful beast. So, in June, they tried again with a harpoon, six men in a boat and another 30 men on the beach to drag the speared animal ashore. Steller's account of the hunting of the sea cow is both dramatic and heart-breaking. The boat prowled among the placid animals and the harpooner struck at a large female. The giant beast churned in the water, the crew's bayonets and knives piercing its gnarled skin, blood spurting as high as a fountain. The herd gallantly rushed to her aid, trying to dislodge the harpoon with their flukes, upturn the boat or bear down on the ropes to snap them. Even after she was dragged ashore lifeless, the sea cow's partner did not give up on her. The following morning he still waited for her close to the shore while she was being butchered on the beach. He was still there on the third day, though her body was mostly gone.

The killing gave Steller the opportunity for a thorough scientific examination, although dissecting a sea cow was tough going. Steller had to contend with the rain, the cold, the tide and, of course, the tenacious foxes that ran off with his notebooks. His comrades, despite owing him their lives, weren't interested in assisting him . . . until they discovered that sea cow intestines could spurt liquid excrement with the pressure of blood from a ruptured vein. 'Not infrequently the face of a spectator would be drenched by this springing fountain as a joke', wrote Steller.

Within the sea cow's carcass Steller found a stomach 'of stupendous size': 1.75 metres (6 feet) long by 1.5 metres (5 feet) wide, so heavy that four strong men hauling it on a rope barely budged it. The entire intestinal tract 'from gullet to anus' was measured at 151 metres (495 feet), over 20 times longer than the living animal.

The castaways now lived like kings. The meat of the sea cow was 'manna from heaven'. It tasted like fine beef and one sea cow could feed the crew for two weeks. Reinvigorated, the men returned to the task of building a new ship. In August, this new *St Peter* set sail from Bering Island. She was a much smaller vessel, but then she had fewer men to carry. The survivors were packed tightly in the hull alongside thousands of valuable otter, fox and seal pelts, and barrels of sea cow meat for the journey home. Steller tried to sneak an entire sea cow skeleton aboard but had to concede there just wasn't room. Just two days later Kamchatka was in sight.

● ● ●

On 27 August 1742, 450 days after 78 men had left in search of America, 46 men returned to Avacha Bay. People were amazed to see them; they had been written off as dead a long time ago, their belongings sold. Others were interested to learn where they had obtained all these sea otter pelts. A mysterious island? Full of animals covered in the finest furs? Stocked with giant floating cows and almost flightless birds? Hunters immediately set their sights on the fur-filled paradise just beyond the horizon. Over the next two decades Bering Island was ransacked; thousands upon thousands of animals were killed. Populations of foxes, otters, fur seals and sea lions were decimated. The spectacled cormorant and Steller's sea cow provided the food that fuelled the slaughter.

Harpooning sea cows from a boat and towing them ashore proved too labour-intensive for the small groups of hunters scattered around the island. Instead, sleeping sea cows were simply skewered with a metal pole. The animals would thrash and flee out to sea where they slowly died. Some of their bodies drifted back to shore where they could be butchered. Most simply drifted away. The last Steller's sea cow was reportedly killed in 1768, just 27 years after Steller discovered them. This magnificent creature had also been discovered on adjacent Copper Island in 1745; they were hunted to extinction here in just nine years. The spectacled cormorant was 'killed in great numbers for food'. The only details we have of the living bird are Steller's brief notes and cooking instructions.

Unaware of the massacre on Bering Island, Steller continued his explorations across Siberia for a few years and prepared his expedition notes, observations and theories. In 1746, he was heading back to St Petersburg where, I'd like to believe, he would have been hailed as one of the greatest naturalists of his era. He never made it. Georg Steller died from a fever in the Siberian town of Tyumen aged 37.

Every word of his prophecy had come true. His body was wrapped in a red robe and buried in a shallow grave in the frozen ground. But even the grave couldn't stop Steller. Local thieves dug him up, stole the red robe and left his body for the wolves. It was recovered and interred again on the edge of the Tara River where the eroding banks exposed the buried skeletons of mighty woolly mammoths. Eventually time and the Tara wore away the riverbank and Steller's bones tumbled, mixed with the mammoths and were swept away.

● ● ●

After his death, some of Steller's notebooks and journals made it back to the Russian Academy of Sciences, where they were translated and published. His accounts of an island inhabited by 10-tonne sea monsters must have raised some scientific eyebrows. It wasn't until the 1840s, over 70 years after the animal was hunted to extinction, that the first sea cow bones were unearthed on Bering Island and Steller's observations were validated. Leonhard Stejneger, who had traced Steller's footsteps on Bering Island and would write an affectionate biography, collected many sea cow skulls and bones in 1882. Stejneger wrote that the sea cows of Bering Island were 'the last survivors of a once more widely distributed species which had been spared because man had not reached their last resort'. Sea cow bones have since been excavated on other islands in the Bering Sea and all along the Aleutian Islands chain. Bones purporting to be from Steller's sea cow have also been discovered in Pleistocene deposits in Japan and dredged from the seafloor of Monterey

Bay south of San Francisco, suggesting that this animal once had a distribution all around the Pacific Rim. Even today, substantial skeletons of Steller's sea cow are still uncovered. In 2017, researchers undertaking a survey of Bering Island's coastline spotted the bleached ribs of a 6 metre/20 foot-long headless sea cow jutting out from the sand.

Skulls, ribs and other pieces of sea cows can be found in around 50 museums across the world. Complete skeletons will almost certainly be composites; jigsaws of unrelated bones assembled from the butchered bodies of Bering Island, some still bearing the scars of axes and flames. But one museum boasts the world's most intact Steller's sea cow, specimen number: 710/1960, B1400.

● ● ●

In the winter the Baltic Sea is home to Steller's eider. This attractive sea duck was discovered by Steller in huge flocks around Bering Island and subsequently named in his honour. From out on deck I scan the waves through my binoculars, but I can't see any. I must be in the wrong corner of the Baltic. Here, in the middle of the Gulf of Finland, is where my journey crosses paths with Steller's. Steller was still Stöller when he passed here in 1734, sailing east on his way to St Petersburg. Now, 285 years later, I'm travelling north on a crowded passenger ferry from Tallinn. So far, it's been a smoother passage than Steller's voyage on the *St Peter*. None of my fellow shipmates are showing signs of scurvy. The only person not looking too healthy is an Estonian man on his stag night dressed as Freddie Mercury, his friends plying him with lager while chanting 'Another

One Bites The Dust'. He's vomiting overboard by the time we arrive in Helsinki.

The Finnish Museum of Natural History is housed in a stately building with a metal moose on the front lawn and two giraffes peering down from the main balcony. While queueing inside the entrance at the ticket booth I glance to my left and I see it. Beyond an African elephant and under a sweeping staircase, double doors open onto a long corridor. In pride of place in the 'History of Bones' exhibition, Steller's sea cow floats a few feet above the checkerboard tiled floor. I'm so mesmerised by it the ticket lady has to knock on the booth's glass window to get my attention and my €15.

You have to stand alongside a sea cow to appreciate the size. They're massive, although at 5.3 metres (17½ feet) this is a small specimen. Helsinki's sea cow is a young male, a rare example which seemingly died naturally and washed ashore on Bering Island before Steller arrived on the tattered *St Peter* in 1741. It rested intact, undiscovered until its exhumation in 1861. Thick ribs hang down off the spine like a picket fence and its strange toothless skull is almost bird-like, with a chunky beak. The most confusing thing is that the world's most complete Steller's sea cow skeleton appears blatantly incomplete. Something is missing. Where are the hands? Its limbs just stop dead at the wrist. Suspended around the sea cow, the skeletons of other marine mammals – seals, dolphins, even the closely related dugong – flaunt their phalanges, their bony fingers mocking the hands-free beast below. In the past, museum curators, assuming the animals' actual appendages had been lost in transit, would fashion and attach plaster hands to their sea cow specimens to 'complete' them. But we learnt from Steller that these handless forelimbs were indeed the 'strangest feature of all'. With 'no traces of fingers' they were 'as an amputated human limb', covered in thickened skin and wirebrush-like bristles with which they scraped algae and seaweed from the rocks. The blunt limbs were used for swimming, bracing against the rocks, walking in the shallows and hugging. Steller regularly observed sea cows 'in the sting of passion' embracing each other face to face. 'I could not observe indications of an admirable intellect', Steller wrote, 'but they indeed have an extraordinary love for one another.'

Steller's words gave life to the sea cow. Without him we'd be left with nothing but bones and our best guesses as to how this bizarre creature lived and why no one had ever found its hands. Standing here, alongside the sea cow, I'm sharing just some of the wonder and confusion that Steller must have felt as he watched these curious creatures swimming peacefully in the shallows off Bering Island on 8 November 1741. In this moment, standing staring at this bizarre bunch of bones, I feel a bit closer to my hero. And for that alone it was worth the journey.

CHAPTER FOUR

Upland Moa

Megalapteryx didinus

GONE: *c.* 1445

I can't figure out the rental car's satnav and I'm lost in a labyrinth of narrow country lanes. I persevere and, a little further along the valley, I'm rewarded with a layby and the reassurance that 'You have arrived at your destination'. Stepping from the car I'm greeted by the sights, sounds and smells of the English countryside – the rolling hills, the lush green patchwork of sheep-grazed fields. Familiar farmland birds flit through the hedgerow: yellowhammers, chaffinches, goldfinches and, somewhere, high in a cloudless blue sky, a skylark sings his little heart out. But there's something wrong with this picture – a glitch in the matrix, an irregularity among all this Englishness. On the wall of a limestone overhang is some ancient graffiti, several centuries old. Painted in charcoal and animal fat are representations of a massive, long-legged bird with a bulky body and a serpentine neck, and a gigantic eagle with outstretched wings. These fantastical creatures aren't from English myths and legends, because this isn't England. This is New Zealand. And once upon a time in New Zealand these monsters were real.

• • •

When I was a boy, my grandad would take me to Saturday morning screenings at the local Odeon where I'd watch wide-eyed as cavemen grappled dinosaurs in movies like *The Land That Time Forgot* and *One Million Years B.C.* As I got older, I learnt the awful truth: humans and dinosaurs had never coexisted on this planet. Raquel Welch and her deerskin bikini had lied to me. I was crushed. Seeking solace in the pages of my extinct animal books, I discovered my own mysterious land forgotten by time.

If the creation of New Zealand were a Saturday morning blockbuster it would go something like this. In the land before time, the supercontinent of Gondwana begins to shatter. Somewhere, down by Australia and Antarctica, another chunk of continental crust decides to split and go it alone with a new identity: Zealandia. The mammals, who are busy evolving, learn of this departing piece of pristine paradise and race to stake their claim, but with one final wrench and a thunderous 'so long, suckers', Zealandia tears itself free. The mammals arrive moments too late. Screeching to a halt on Australia's eastern edge they shake their fists yelling, 'You haven't seen the last of us Zealandia, we'll be back', but their threats are lost beneath the crashing waves. All they can do is watch as the renegade landmass sails off towards the horizon. Eventually Zealandia settles, isolated in an empty ocean, cools down and almost completely sinks under the waves but triumphantly rises again, buoyed up by tectonic forces and violent volcanism. Today 7 per cent of Zealandia remains above water. Well, those are the edited highlights; the full director's cut lasts 80 million years.

The largest part of Zealandia's defiant 7 per cent, New Zealand, was a land without land mammals. Sure, there were a few bats, the beaches were crowded with seals and sea lions, and whales and dolphins swam round its shores, but the forests, swamps and mountains remained mammal-free. While other continents had their deer, bison, giraffes and elephants, all New Zealand had was a vacancy, an exciting opportunity for some large herbivores to take advantage of the lush vegetation that was standing around uneaten. Without any mammalian applicants that job went to the birds.

Until recently, it was assumed that the moa had always been on New Zealand, the descendant of a flightless Gondwanan bird, a stowaway separatist on Zealandia. However, recent genetic and morphological research has revealed something surprising. The moa's closest relatives are tinamou, chicken-sized birds from South America which are able to fly. Millions of years ago, ancient ancestors of the moa and tinamou flew to New Zealand, where they found abundant food and, in the absence of mammals, freedom on the forest floor. Without the pressure of predators, these birds no longer needed to hide and escape. So, they stopped flying, lost their wings and grew big. Very big.

As a boy I would read about the moa and dream that one day I might visit the exotic, distant islands of New Zealand. But now that I'm here, driving down the east coast of the South Island, it all feels so bloody familiar, so. . . English. Since the nineteenth century, European settlers have converted New Zealand into a replica of England – the fields, farms, bungalows, roundabouts, fish and chip shops. The English even brought their wildlife with them; the telegraph wires are full of starlings, the roads paved with squashed hedgehogs. It feels like I've travelled so far around the world that I'm right back where I started. At least the city of Dunedin doesn't look English. It looks Scottish.

● ● ●

Kane Fleury has the coolest job in the world; he gets to hang out with the moa. Dunedin's Otago Museum boasts one of the world's largest collections of articulated moa skeletons, and Kane, assistant curator of natural sciences, has offered to give me the tour. 'Moa bones helped build this museum', Kane tells me as we pass under the fin whale skeleton suspended above one of the museum's original Victorian galleries. 'The Otago region was home to many different moa species and was a rich source of their remains. Every museum around the world wanted moa bones, so our surplus bones were used as currency and occasionally traded for other exhibits.'

The museum's moa exhibition is arranged so you can stand among them and feel part of this skeletal flock. The nine moa species of New Zealand ranged wildly in size. The baby of the bunch, the turkey-sized little bush moa, stood 90 centimetres (36 inches) tall at the back and weighed 25 kilograms (55 pounds). Eastern and stout-legged moa were possibly the loudest species, with specially adapted looping windpipes. 'We can only guess the sort of sounds they produced', says Kane, although he isn't willing to demonstrate in a crowded museum. Heavy-footed, crested and Mantell's moa were bizarre-looking beasts. These dumpy moas had short, stout legs, which supported a bulky body – presumably packed with the extensive intestines required to digest woody vegetation. Then we have the real showstoppers: the North Island giant moa and South Island giant moa. I stand dwarfed in the shadow of the musuem's South Island giant moa skeleton. The females of these two species weighed up to 250 kilograms (550 pounds) and stood 2 metres (7 feet) tall at their back, the height of a doorframe. They could stretch their neck to reach up to an unbelievable 3.5 metres (12 feet): the tallest birds ever known.

Kane shows me his favourite moa exhibit: the skeleton of an upland moa discovered by hunters in a cave in the

Serpentine Range in 2002. Among the bones was an almost intact, unlaid pale green egg, which has now been respectfully restored to its rightful position within mother moa's reconstructed skeleton. Upland moa were relatively small and agile, possessing large slender toes, an adaption for walking across snowy subalpine habitats. Kane highlights the skeleton's posture: 'Many museum moa are posed with their necks erect to exaggerate their height. Have you been out tramping in the bush yet?', asks Kane, 'it's so dense, moa wouldn't have got far walking round like that.' This skeleton's posture, with its snaked neck slung low in front of the body, typifies their natural stance.

The exhibit that I really want to see lies in the shadows of a side room under strictly controlled humidity and temperature, one of the world's best-preserved moa remains: the mummified leg of an upland moa. The leg had lain preserved by the dry air of a Central Otago mountain cave for centuries and looks so deceptively fresh that Kane could've convinced me it was from a moa that died last month. Dense, thin feathers still cover its thigh, muscles and tissue still hang from the bone and its scaly foot with bleached, hooked claws is pure velociraptor.

I say goodbye to Kane. The next time I see him he's on a TV news report diverting a river in order to rescue moa footprints preserved in the riverbed. See, I told you he had a cool job. Outside the museum's café stands a fibreglass model, a mystic moa who will tell you her secrets if you donate a dollar. I deposit my coin, her eyes flash green and I lean in close as her voice confides the moa's deepest fear: 'We were scared of the Haast's eagle.'

● ● ●

With lots of herbivores standing around uneaten, New Zealand now had another vacancy: an exciting opportunity for an apex predator. Elsewhere in the world that job would have gone to a mammal, a lion or a wolf perhaps, but in New Zealand the successful applicant was another bird, one that, at first, didn't seem up to the job. Less than 2.5 million years ago, a small eagle arrived in New Zealand and, faced with a multitude of meaty moa, it evolved relatively rapidly into a bird 10 times its original size, the Haast's eagle. Named after German explorer Julius von Haast, this colossal bird of prey possessed a wingspan of 3 metres (10 feet) and weighed up to 17.7 kilograms (39 pounds) – twice the weight of our current heaviest eagle, Steller's sea eagle (named after another German explorer, our friend Georg Steller). Haast's eagle became the nemesis of even the largest moa. Mutilated moa bones indicate this killer swooped down on unsuspecting moa, floored them and, with powerful talons the size of a tiger's claws, punctured their pelvis and shattered their skulls. It must have been a sight to see. The moa now had to be wary and keep one eye on the sky. And they had to watch where they were stepping too.

I place one foot gingerly in front of the other and don't look down. I really don't feel comfortable on wobbly rope bridges. Yet here I am, teetering and terrified, halfway across a ravine deep in the lush fern-filled forests of the South Island's Oparara Basin. I reach the far side and am just reacquainting myself with solid ground when my guide, Bill Jackson, hands me a helmet and head torch and leads me down into it. I'm not particularly comfortable in caves either and I hesitantly stumble and grope my way along the dank, cold cave wall while Bill cheerily highlights some of the geological features carved by water and time. The subterranean maze of Honeycomb Hill cave is named after its 70 openings, which permit sparkling shafts of sunshine to pierce the pitch darkness. Those openings also acted as pitfall traps for the moa. 'Since explorers discovered these caves in 1976, they've carted two tonnes of bones out of here, most of them moa from six different species', Bill informs me as his torchlight beam prowls the cave floor, picking out moa bones among the limestone slabs. 'There must be many more tonnes buried under there.' Bill spotlights the full skeleton of a little bush moa pieced together on a cave ledge. 'The scientists tell me the bones found here date from 600 to 20,000 years old. Or maybe older. You know what scientists are like; never make up their bloody minds.'

A few days later, I join a busy tourist tour of the Ngarua Caves below Takaka Hill. While the group stares up at the impressive illuminated stalactites, my eyes are fixed on the crested moa skeleton sprawled on the cave floor. Our guide, Charmaine, informs us the bird's carbon-dated bones reveal it dropped into this cave around 22,900 BC. She crouches, asking, 'Do any kids here want to hold a moa bone?' I can't miss this opportunity. As she passes a chunky femur among the children, I sneak around the back of the group and kneel down in an attempt to pass myself off as a heavily bearded eight-year-old. It works. I'm passed the bone and, holding it, I feel a connection to the moa that fell here 24,918 years ago. But mostly I feel a connection to a boy from 40 years ago who dreamt of growing up to one day be a guy kneeling in a cave in New Zealand with a moa bone in his hands.

• • •

It would be a slow, easy life for the moa if they could just avoid holes in the ground, treacherous swamps and fearsome eagles. These extraordinary birds ruled the roost for millions of years in a strange lost world dominated by birds. And then, one day, from across the eastern ocean, the future finally caught up with them. 'Hey Zealandia, remember us?'

Over the past 80 million years the mammals had been busy. Some had even learnt how to stand up, use their hands and build boats. Humans eventually discovered New Zealand sometime around 1300. The scene was set for one of history's epic confrontations as men stepped from their three-keeled boats and into the ring. Ladies and gentlemen, in the blue corner, the homegrown heroes, weighing in at 500 pounds, the 'kegs on legs': the moa. And in the red corner, our challengers, from 2,000 miles across the sea, 160 pounds of pure Polynesian, the humans. On paper, I'd have put my money on the moa, but this fight was fixed. The moa were slow, docile and without fear of their opponent; you could probably have just walked up to one and whacked it over the head. The first settlers of New Zealand, the Māori, were hungry and heavily armed – a lethal combination. Under clubs and spears, traps and snares, the moa fell. Hunters carried the birds' bodies to communal processing plants, where they were carved up, the meat distributed among tribes and the discarded bones piled high in middens, the kitchen's waste heaps.

Where New Zealand State Highway 1 crosses the wide Waitaki River I pull over to stretch my legs. Here on the shoreline over 1,000 middens and open ovens have been unearthed, containing the bones of up to 90,000 moa. Such sites were located at the mouths of most rivers around New Zealand. I continue south, cruising the coastline beyond Oamaru searching for another Māori moa hunting site: Awamoa. I'm about to give up until I round the headland and I'm greeted by the 'Old Bones' hotel and a 3-metre (10-foot) model of a moa standing in the middle of a field. This could be the place.

The man who excavated this site came from a family of famous fossil hunters. Walter Mantell was the son of Gideon and Mary Mantell and in 1839, aged 19, he left Sussex seeking a new life in New Zealand. After securing employment, Walter would head out on optimistic expeditions into the islands' wild interior in search of living moa, unaware that he was four centuries too late. In November 1852, Gideon died after taking an overdose of opium to end years of crippling pain following a carriage accident on Clapham Common. The following month, his son Walter was discovering a 'most copious harvest' of moa remains among the buried middens of Awamoa. Walter even dug some charcoal from a Māori oven and used it to cook his pork and eels, joking that it gave his meal 'an exquisite moa flavour'. On 29 December 1852, Walter Mantell stood right here and sketched the scene in front of him. I unfold an A4 printout of Walter's drawing and, holding it at arm's length, I line up the peaks of the distant mountain range. Those summits are still there, but missing from the scene today are the five men Walter drew tottering their way down the creek, engulfed under the huge packs strapped to their backs – packs filled with hundreds of moa bones bound for London.

I clasp my red backpack tightly to my chest and stare at my reflection in the carriage window as I hurtle through the tunnels of the London Underground. A month after I had returned from New Zealand, I attended a local ornithological meeting; over tea and biscuits I had been telling a fellow bird-watcher about my travels, when out of the blue he asked, 'Would you like a moa bone? I have one in the back of a drawer at home.' I stood in disbelief, my digestive half-dunked. 'A what?' 'A moa bone, you know, a bone from a moa. I was given it years ago when a museum was having a clear out. You'd probably appreciate it more than I do. Do you want it?'

My mantelpiece was hastily cleared of sentimental ornaments and framed family photographs, a perspex display case was delivered and the TV abandoned as I sat on the sofa and binge-watched a bird bone. The bone is 35 centimetres (15 inches) long, dark tan in colour and chipped at one end, allowing a glimpse into the dense honeycomb structure within. It appears smooth but, at certain angles, sunlight reveals several scars and a rough, reticulated pattern, as if one side has been seared by flames. I had solemnly accepted responsibility for the bone as if I'd been entrusted with Excalibur and, as the current bone custodian, I felt it my duty to find out more about it.

I undo the zip on my red backpack and snake my hand inside to reassure myself that my precious cargo is safe. Grasping the moa bone I imagine it forming inside a huge egg centuries before, then slowly growing within a ponderous bird roaming mountainous forests. I think of a brutal death, the spear, the hunter, the butchered body, the feast for a tribe under southern stars. And now here it is, rattling along the Circle Line between Sloane Square and South Kensington. Transporting a moa bone across London is a stressful experience these days. Every commuter in this compartment is a potential bone thief. Earlier, at Victoria Station, when a police patrol approached, I froze. I expected a giant bone would be more distracting to two sniffer dogs than cocaine or Semtex. I'm relieved when I eventually reach my destination and step inside the Natural History Museum. 'Can I just check inside your bag, sir?' The security guard ushers me to a table, where I sheepishly unzip my backpack. After some raised eyebrows and a plausible explanation, 'I'm taking the bone to a curator to learn more about it', I'm allowed inside. I suppose walking into the Natural History Museum with a giant bone looks a lot less suspicious than walking out with one.

Once inside I turn and face Hintze Hall, the immense grand gallery that welcomes you to the museum. For a few moments I stand stupefied, overwhelmed by its scale and splendour, just as I had when I first visited this wondrous building as a child. Each archway, alcove and staircase beckons with the promise of some thrilling exhibit. Before I can decide which to choose, I'm surrounded by a sea of schoolchildren who shriek and swirl around me. I wade towards the sanctuary of a *Mantellisaurus*, the iguanodon-like dinosaur named after Gideon Mantell, but get swept towards the gift shop. A door slides open, an empty lift beckons invitingly and I ascend to the first floor. It's calmer here, but as I turn, I come face to face with a sinister-looking figure standing in the shadows: another man carrying a moa bone.

• • •

The blackened bronze statue of Richard Owen looms over me, a moa bone in his outstretched left hand. I'm surprised to meet Owen here, because when I last saw him a decade ago, he was over there, basking in the sunlight at the top of the staircase, presiding over Hintze Hall. That position is now taken by Charles Darwin. People queue to take selfies with Darwin while he sits smiling like some benevolent Father Christmas in his enchanted grotto of evolution – the Gandalf to Richard Owen's dark Saruman. The statues of these naturalists swapped places in 2008, returning Darwin to the best seat in the house as his 200th birthday present. But no one is in a rush to swap them back. That's because no one likes Richard Owen.

That Owen was a brilliant anatomist is not in question. His understanding of the physical differences and similarities between species was rivalled only by the great Georges Cuvier himself. Owen was at the top of his game at a time when Europeans were exploring the globe and making incredible natural history discoveries. Everybody sought his judgment and he therefore became the man who first described and named hundreds of new species. And let's not forget it was Owen's idea to build the Natural History Museum, his 'cathedral to Nature'.

He may have been an anatomical genius but it is hard not to cast Owen as the villain in our story. Highly ambitious and competitive, he used whatever devious means available to derail and discredit those he perceived as rivals to ensure he received all the fame and glory. His vendetta against Gideon Mantell was legendary. Even after Mantell died, Owen didn't stop tormenting him; he wrote a scathing anonymous obituary discrediting his achievements and even kept a portion of poor Gideon's badly injured spine in a jar to showcase its severe deformity. I'll allow Gideon Mantell to have the last word here on Richard Owen: 'a pity a man so talented should be so dastardly and envious'.

I'm not the first person to carry a moa bone across London. That man was Dr John Rule and, on 18 October 1839, Rule was carrying the first moa bone ever to reach Europe. Like me, he was seeking the opinion of an expert. Initially that expert, Richard Owen, didn't have time to waste on some stranger with a worthless chunk of marrowbone, but Rule urged him to look closer. This bone was special.

That very bone, an underwhelming 15-centimetre (6-inch) fractured fragment of a femur, is now on display in Hintze Hall. I crouch, peering up through its hollow shaft, a tunnel with honeycombed walls. On 12 November 1839, Richard Owen carried this bone to Leicester Square for the fortnightly meeting of the Zoological Society of London. Forty-three years earlier, Cuvier had taken to the stage in Paris and magicked up the mighty mammoth and mastodon from bare bones. Now Owen captivated a room of spellbound scientists as he drew their attention to the broken femur's anatomical intricacies and, before their very eyes, he conjured up a bird from a bone. A very big bird. Owen declared that there once existed, or maybe even still existed, a bird in the distant land of New Zealand that may even be equal to the size of an ostrich. To underline his conviction, he staked his reputation on it.

It would go down in history as a career-defining moment, the night the great Richard Owen used his genius osteological insights to resurrect the moa from a single scrap of evidence. What is often forgotten is that the man who gave him the bone, Dr John Rule, told him that it came from a giant extinct bird from New Zealand. Owen was more than happy to take all the accolade. Now, with his reputation on the line, Owen waited for more evidence of his 'gigantic bird of New Zealand' to appear. Three years later the first crates of vindication started arriving in London.

I have an appointment with Sandra Chapman, curator of fossil reptiles and birds, and I wait for her under a giant sloth. Sandra appears just in time to rescue me from an oncoming swarm of schoolchildren and leads me to the calm of a museum storeroom. While opening the first cabinet, Sandra tells me that moa specimens represent around one-third of the Natural History Museum's fossil bird collection. She shows me the remains from a variety of different moa species as well as some bonus bones of the great auk excavated from Funk Island's thick topping of guano. 'Frustratingly, many of the moa bones that made it to England were not labelled', Sandra says, 'so the precise where and when of their discovery is a mystery'. Which reminds me. I reach into my backpack and pull out my precious moa bone. Can Sandra tell me anything about it? 'Well, it *is* a moa bone', Sandra confirms, which is a relief. I could have been sat staring at an ostrich bone for the past month (not that I have anything against ostriches, of course). 'It's a femur', she continues, 'and quite well preserved. The peat it has been buried in would have given it this dark colouration.' Can she identify what species it belongs to? Unfortunately, not. Sandra explains 'there are just too many variables due to age and sex'. Female moas were substantially bigger than the males, in some species 150 per cent taller and 280 per cent heavier. The sheer variety of different-sized moa bones that arrived in Victorian England from New Zealand prompted Richard Owen to propose that there were 18 moa species, while Walter Rothschild believed there were 37. By the year 2000, scientists had whittled down the moa to 11 species, then 10 in 2006 and 9 in 2009.

Many crates of moa bones arrived in Victorian England from excavations of Māori middens across New Zealand. The bones from the 1852 Awamoa excavations sat unopened in the British Museum until Walter Mantell himself visited England in 1856 and unpacked them under the watchful eye of Richard Owen. Within those crates were the first identified bones of the heavy-footed moa, which would later be reconstructed and stand on display in the museum alongside the giant sloth and mastodon. Mantell and Owen also unpacked eggshell fragments – jigsaw pieces which, when painstakingly pieced together, re-created a dozen enormous moa eggs. The Awamoa discoveries were 'unmistakable proof', said Mantell, 'of the harmonious coexistence of man with the moa'. It is a peculiar observation because 'harmonious' and 'coexistence' are the exact two words I would never use when describing the relationship between man and moa.

• • •

I walk across the bridge over the creek at Awamoa and stand staring up at the life-size statue of a South Island giant moa. I'm still staggered by the concept of a bird

1.25 metres (4 feet) taller t[...] moa was equally unbelieva[...] while England and France [...] and Europe fell to the P[...] the moa. And the moa w[...] colonisation of New Ze[...] blitzkrieg. Humans slau[...] killing young and old ar[...] dogs would have savag[...] up to a decade to reacl[...] two eggs each year, the[...] survive this onslaught. [...] after humans arrived [...] were extinct. Haast's [...] food, died with then[...]

There were thos[...] wipe out an entire r[...] research undertake[...] Allentoft of the U[...] the last 4,000 year[...] been stable, even i[...] of their pending [...] 'The moa are th[...]

I climb back [...] road, heading n[...] statue of the gi[...] just like the m[...]

CHAPTER FIVE

Huia

Heteralocha acutirostris

GONE: *c.* 1925

They can remember a girl, possibly fair-haired, slipping past the office door and out of the museum. Nothing particularly unusual. It was only when they entered the main exhibition room an hour later that they discovered what had happened. The side screws had been removed, the display cabinet prised open. Inside, a glossy black bird stood perched alongside its partner just as it had for over a century. Except now the bird's tail feathers were plucked, stolen, gone. In death, just as in life, the huia was being hunted.

● ● ●

Of all the extinct animals in this book, it's the huia that I miss the most. As a child I fell in love with these extraordinary birds the moment I saw the vintage painting of two huia that graced the cover of my favourite book, Errol Fuller's *Extinct Birds*. The huia was everything I wanted in a bird: unique, exotic and odd. Like the moa it had lived in New Zealand, and I'd often lie on my bed dreaming of those faraway forests where the huia once flew.

Huia are members of the family Callaeatidae, the New Zealand wattlebirds, five species named after the brightly coloured fleshy adornments that droop down on either side of their jaw. The huia's wattles were bright orange, a jolt of colour on an otherwise black, sleek body which glistened with a glossy blue iridescence. Twelve long tail feathers were tipped pure white, a feature particularly noticeable when the bird displayed to its partner, spreading these feathers into a fan. Their legs were relatively long, their wings noticeably short and rounded. Huia could fly short distances but preferred travelling through the forest by hopping along the ground or leaping acrobatically from branch to branch.

There was something wonderfully weird about the huia. When I describe birds, I'm always uncertain when to use the word 'beak' as opposed to the word 'bill', so I usually deal with this on a bird-by-bird basis. The huia is the only bird I can explain using both. The male huia had a definite *beak*: robust, pointed, like a chunky pickaxe. The female huia, on the other hand, possessed something totally different, what I could only call a *bill*: long, slender and decurved. A few other bird species show a slight difference in beak/bill structure between the sexes, but none have taken it to the extremes of the huia. Armed with such wildly different tools, both birds could exploit different niches within the same habitat, so weren't in direct competition for food. While the male's pickaxe beak hacked forcefully at dead wood to excavate beetle grubs, the female would use her long, delicate bill like a pair of forceps, clinically probing and extracting grubs and insects from deep crevices. Some observers claimed the birds would work together, sharing their spoils between them.

Huia were only found on New Zealand's North Island, where excavations of prehistoric sites indicate they were once widespread. They lived within the dark heart of the ancient forests, travelling together in the shadows of the towering tōtara and rimu trees. Huia always came as a pair; they couldn't bear to be apart. Oh, and in case you're struggling, it's pronounced 'hoo-ee-ah'; I just thought I'd wait a few paragraphs and let you have a go for yourself.

• • •

To the indigenous people of New Zealand, the huia became 'king of the leaves and sky' and held an important place in Māori culture. Only the highest-ranking Māori were allowed to wear the huia's white-tipped tail feather in their hair, and this elite status was conferred on the bird itself. As a sacred bird, hunting was restricted to certain seasons. Hunters would imitate the bird's whistling call, luring the inquisitive huia to where a noose on a pole would be waiting and slipped over the bird's head. Its distress calls would undoubtedly lure its mate to a similar fate. Huia skins were carefully dried, their heads strung together as pendants, the hallowed tail feathers plucked and stored in intricately carved wooden caskets (*waka huia*). Feathers were donned by Māori chiefs as a show of status at ceremonies; all twelve huia plumes worn together created a *marereko* – the headdress of war.

By 1840, when Europeans started settling in New Zealand, the bird was only encountered in the southern forests of the North Island. At this time the Māori's rules protecting the sacred huia began to crumble. Now it seemed everyone could wear a huia feather, regardless of status, and the killing of the bird became increasingly indiscriminate. Imperious European settlers might have mocked the curious Māori custom of using bird ornaments to express social status, but when collectors back in Europe learnt about the huia, the bird with two beaks, everyone wanted a posed pair in their parlour to impress their own social circles. This fresh demand from wealthy European collectors, museums and zoos caused the hunting to intensify. Thousands of huia, alive and dead, were shipped back to Europe where they were held in high esteem by Victorian society.

• • •

All that Walter Buller craved was to be held in high esteem by Victorian society. Born in New Zealand in 1838, Buller's birthplace was the chip on his shoulder and he became a driven man, desperate for acknowledgment and respect from his European-born peers. But his New Zealand heritage gave him one advantage over all of them: an extensive knowledge of his country's wildlife. Buller became the 'father of New Zealand ornithology'. His greatest achievements were the two glorious editions of *A History of the Birds of New Zealand* (published in 1873 and 1888), a book so good even the famously malicious Richard Owen had something nice to say about it. The book's iconic huia illustration, by John Gerrard Keulemans, is still encountered in gift shops across the country, allowing the huia to live on in the hearts, minds and tea towels of the New Zealand people.

I've tried to like Walter Buller, I really have, but he was certainly a complicated man. Buller was also the man best placed to supply information and specimens to naturalists in Europe, and this is where he has acquired his reputation as something of a villain.

Through his evocative writing, Buller breathed life into the huia and taught us most of what we know about the bird, but some paragraphs are a rollercoaster of emotions. He'll describe the birds with obvious affection – 'they were caressing each other with their beautiful bills'– then, in the same sentence, his companion raises his gun and, 'a charge of No. 6 brought both to the ground together'. Buller then expresses remorse – 'The incident was rather touching, and I felt almost glad that the shot was not mine' – before rubbing his hands and gleefully concluding he was 'by no means loth to appropriate two fine specimens'.

Today Buller's accounts of huia hunting are difficult to read, although Buller only killed around 30 huia during his life. This was at a time when one hunting party reportedly killed almost 650 huia in a single month. As early as 1840, German naturalist Ernst Dieffenbach encountered four huia and warned that the bird's extinction 'may not be far distant'. And to hasten his point he shot three of them. But much more insidious threats than 'a charge of No. 6' faced the huia.

● ● ●

I'm driving south under blue skies on State Highway 2. As far as the eye can see there are the lush grazing pastures and agricultural fields that dominate the lower east side of the North Island. Not too long ago, this area of New Zealand was part of the Seventy Mile Bush – a vast, dark, impenetrable forest of ancient trees and giant tree ferns. In 1872, 21 families from Denmark and Norway arrived here and founded the settlement of Dannevirke, which explains why I'm greeted by a 3-metre (10-foot) Viking as I enter the town. The burly Scandinavian settlers allotted the forests between them and then got to work 'scrubbing the bush', felling and firing huge tracts of this pristine landscape. The sky turned black as the lowlands burned. Sawmills were established to process the timber, and grass seeds were sown among the ashes. Gradually the untameable forest became regimented grazing pastures. A similar story played out all across New Zealand, the pioneers' clearances destroying the forest homes of the huia and many other native birds. The destruction of these lowland forests also deprived the huia of the winter-feeding areas that were essential for birds forced down from the mountains during colder weather. Here, around Dannevirke, the huia were forced to retreat west to the Ruahine Range, where the forested mountains remained too rugged to tame. But even the familiar shadows of the remaining ancient forests were no longer a refuge.

The huia, like the moa and all of New Zealand's native birds, had evolved in a land without any mammalian predators. They could safely forage on the forest floor and nest close to the ground without the threat of something fanged and furry sneaking up on them. That had all changed when Polynesian boats first landed in New Zealand around 1300, unwittingly bringing with them Pacific rats. And now, 500 years later, European settlers and passing whaling boats continuously added their own sinister stowaways: Norway rats and ship rats.

The settlers also purposely imported a much greater evil: the rabbit. These blameless bunnies were imported for food, for hunting or just to remind folks of home. Without predators, the rabbit population swelled to plague proportions, nibbling the precious new pastures and undercutting the sheep. Farmers were furious, but the solution seemed simple: import some predators. Naturalists raised objections (Walter Buller was noticeably quiet on the subject), but a democratic vote was taken, mainly by the sheep farmers. And so, in 1882, the government began importing and releasing stoats, weasels and ferrets. One naturalist recalled 'seeing crates full of stoats and weasels in the yard behind the government building when they were first imported', adding, 'had I possessed an inkling of what they were to mean to our native birdlife I do not think any of them would have escaped out of those crates alive'. The tenacious rats, stoats and the other imported mammals discovered an all-you-can-eat buffet of naive native birds, all physically and behaviourally unprepared for this tidal wave of sharp teeth. They didn't stand a chance, and the forests fell silent.

• • •

I pull up outside my destination, the Dannevirke Gallery of History, only to discover it closed an hour ago. I've travelled a long way to get here but not once did I consider checking the opening times. I curse myself for being an idiot. However, a note in the window suggests that idiots like me should phone Nancy. Five minutes later, Nancy Wadsworth, the gallery's president and one of a team of dedicated volunteers who staff this wonderful, rural museum, arrives and cheerfully lets me in. Inside I find exhibitions dedicated to the town's Scandinavian heritage, photos of the fire that swept through Dannevirke's high street a century ago and an extensive collection of pens embossed with the names of local businesses. But there's only one display I'm here to see.

In 2012, an online report of the theft of a huia's tail feathers from a small museum on the other side of the world had reacquainted me with the bird I fell in love with as a child. And it ultimately led me here, years later, on a pilgrimage to the very scene of the crime. Now I stand solemnly before the glass-fronted case containing two beautiful black birds. This pair of huia are believed to have been the last ever seen in the Pohangina Valley, north-west of Dannevirke. Shot in 1889, they were given as a wedding gift – for what better way is there to wish newlyweds every happiness than by wiping out a local population of an endangered bird? As we stand in the empty exhibition hall, Nancy relates the events of that day in 2012 when a possibly fair-haired thief forced open the huia's display case and stole the male's tail. The local newspaper had reported that museum staff had been left 'devastated' and 'sickened'. The town's police sergeant said their community had 'lost part of our heritage, our history'. Dr Colin Miskelly, from Te Papa, New Zealand's incredible national museum, called it 'an example of personal greed … no different to the theft of medals from a military museum'. 'The female's tail was intact but ruffled', Nancy recalls, 'maybe the thief was disturbed as they tried to remove them too.' The male huia within has since been restored. 'He was sent away and his tail was replaced with coloured turkey feathers', Nancy explains. A note alongside the case mentions the theft and admits the display's 'authenticity has been compromised'. Reading it reminded me that the same greed that destroyed the huia a century ago is still loose in the world today. 'The gallery wishes visitors to know this fact.'

• • •

'It doesn't surprise me', says Dr Colin Miskelly. It's a few days later and I'm 160 kilometres (100 miles) south and a few metres underground. I'm reminding Colin of the theft of a fistful of feathers from Dannevirke as I follow him down through a series of security doors to a basement storeroom somewhere underneath Wellington. Colin is one of New Zealand's leading ornithologists and conservationists, founder of the exhaustive *NZ Birds Online* website and curator of vertebrates at Te Papa. I'm still babbling about the theft as we approach a tall metal cabinet in the corner of a room filled with tall metal cabinets. 'Well, like I said', Colin interjects, 'it doesn't surprise me.' He opens the doors and slides out a metal drawer. Lying on the tray, like cadavers in a mortuary, are figures which at first I don't recognise. They are huia. But they are different, deformed, desecrated. They have no tails. Another tray contains more specimens, either tail-less or with just a few of their tail feathers remaining. Many huia specimens donated to the museum's collection have arrived without their tails. The obsession with huia feathers has never really ended, Colin explains, a financial value now replacing their cultural significance. At an auction in 2010, a determined phone bidder purchased a single huia tail feather for NZ$8,000 (around £4,000), a world-record price for a feather. Today, huia feathers still occasionally appear on New Zealand's internet auction sites.

Colin opens another cabinet and I'm wowed by an entire flock of huia, posed and perched, their tails intact. Te Papa holds about 40 huia skins. 'They're New Zealand's commonest extinct bird', Colin says before showing me something very unique, the only known huia egg in the world – a fragment of cracked eggshell resting on a bed of cotton wool. There's another unique relic held by Te Papa that I'm also interested in. The museum holds the iguanodon tooth discovered by Mary and Gideon Mantell in Sussex, which was later brought to New Zealand by their son, Walter. I ask if I can see this iconic fossil, but Colin explains it's unfortunately unavailable today. I wonder if he's been warned to be wary of suspicious Englishmen who may be seeking to repatriate it. Well, it would certainly look great in Mantell's display case back at the Booth Museum.

By the 1890s, the huia was facing extinction from the relentless onslaught of guns, rats, cats, stoats and weasels. They needed a hero, someone to stand up for them. However, their saviour, when he finally arrived, could barely stand up on his own. Fifteen-month old Victor Onslow, the son of the governor of New Zealand, had been baptised with the name of the Māori's sacred bird as his middle name. It was a shrewd, well-publicised gesture that had won the hearts of all New Zealanders, who would forever know him as Huia Onslow. The man who had suggested the name was Walter Buller, who, to endear himself further to the governor, took a sudden interest in the huia's conservation and arranged a meeting between Māori tribal leaders and the young child. The Māori beseeched Governor Onslow to grant protection for their sacred bird so 'when your boy grows up he may see the beautiful bird that bears his name'. The huia received official protection in 1892 and the proclamation was signed by 15-month-old Huia Onslow (well, it's more of a squiggle than a signature). But even as Buller arranged for the bird's protection with one hand, with the other he was ordering hunting parties into the forests to find him more huia specimens.

Stoats and weasels weren't the only menace arriving from Britain. On 15 June 1901, the Duke of York, the man who would become King George V, paid a royal visit to the geothermal town of Rotorua on the North Island. On that day, the duke inadvertently signed the huia's death warrant. His Māori guide, Maggie, greeted the duke and, as a sign of respect to his status, bestowed upon his royal hat a white-tipped tail feather from a vanishing bird. It sat in his brim, for all to see, in the pages of newspapers around the world. The huia now became fashion victims. Oblivious of their protection, there was a period of renewed hunting as everyone from Auckland to London wanted this feather in their cap.

It seemed that it was all over for the huia. But there was one final hope. A promising new idea had been proposed, which was now gaining momentum. Could threatened birds like the huia be captured and relocated to start new populations on offshore, predator-free island sanctuaries? These islands would be the lifeboats for birds whose populations were sinking as New Zealand's North and South Islands became submerged under wave upon wave of introduced predators. In 1902, this rescue operation gained government approval, but its delivery, led by three separate government departments, was a bungled mess. At one point three huia were captured and caged for release on Kapiti Island, but after no one turned up to collect them, they were liberated back into the forest. Another government-funded hunter captured two live huia, which were destined for Little Barrier Island, another predator-free haven. Could this pair save the entire species from extinction?

Walter Buller had a better idea. Why waste these valuable birds on a conservation project? A wealthy acquaintance of Buller's in England was looking for two specimens of the huia for his new menagerie. 'My dear Rothschild,' wrote Buller, 'I have at length, I am delighted to say, obtained a beautiful pair of live huia for you.'

In his Tring menagerie Walter Rothschild no doubt rubbed his big hands in delight.

Buller bent the law, intercepted the pair and had them shipped off to England. There is no evidence they ever arrived.

• • •

I annually forget the birthdays of my friends and family, but 28 December has been indelibly etched in my mind since I was a child. On this date each year I commemorate the fact that in 1907 Mr Walter William Smith stood in the Tararua Mountains and watched the last ever huia as they flew out of sight forever. Smith's sighting has always been cited as the extinction date for the huia, any sightings reported after this date discounted, regardless of their veracity. In 2017, Ross Galbreath published some detailed detective work. He traced W.W. Smith's movements and concluded he couldn't have been where he said he was on 28 December 1907. This sighting should therefore be classed as unreliable. And why was this the 'last sighting' anyway? There were some particularly convincing huia sightings on the eastern side of Wellington Harbour up until the 1920s. On one occasion huia were even photographed, although this tantalising evidence – the only alleged photos of the huia – was subsequently lost. In 2016, ecologist Nikki McArthur was digitising data from old ornithological notebooks and came across a previously unreported huia sighting from 1924, when a shepherd attracted an inquisitive huia while whistling for his dogs at the edge of the Akatarawa Forest. It seems reasonable that the huia hung on until the 1920s. After this, sightings become less reliable (although a convincing pair of CGI huia were rediscovered in New Zealand filmmaker Taika Waititi's 2016 movie *Hunt for the Wilderpeople*).

We are left with a shattered egg, stuffed specimens and skins scattered across the globe. But something else has survived. The song of the huia. Possibly. The bird was never photographed or recorded, but in 1949 Robert Batley had the remarkable foresight to sit down with Hēnare Hāmana , an elderly Māori huia hunter who once lured in the huia by imitating their call. The acetate disc crackles and Hēnare whistles the lonesome song of the Huia: 'uia, uia, uia' 'where are you?', 'where are you?'

● ● ●

In the shadows of the majestic rimu and miro trees, the stream bends and the water slows and deepens. Out where the Ōrongorongo River winds through the forested ridges of the Remutaka Ranges, George Gibbs, who until now has been setting an impressive pace along the track, stops and pauses. A broad smile widens on his face: 'This is huia country.' Just a few hours earlier George had been waiting for me as my water taxi pulled in on the eastern shore of Wellington Harbour. I was already indebted to George. His book *Ghosts of Gondwana* had been my introduction to the evolution of life in New Zealand. A renowned naturalist, George follows in the footsteps of his grandfather George Hudson, one of New Zealand's pioneer entomologists. In

1895, Hudson, who worked as a shift-worker at Wellington's Post Office, was so desperate for a few extra hours of daylight in which he could search for insects that he proposed the idea of 'daylight savings time'. It caught on and, 125 years later, we're all still thrown into mild confusion twice a year as we change our clocks to accommodate Hudson's hobby. Young George, his grandson, would try to keep up with his enthusiastic grandfather on these collecting trips, watching him as he filled his suit pockets with pots and pillboxes, beetles and butterflies.

Today it's my turn to try and keep up as George and his wife Keena enthusiastically tramp along the Remutaka Ranges' Catchpool Track. I had asked George if he would take me to a place I had dreamt of as a child, the place where the huia once were. George had handed me our treasure map – a clipping from Wellington's *Evening Post*, dated Friday, 5 February 1937. Under the headline 'Beautiful Songsters Now Extinct', the article contains the recollections of A.H. Messenger and a hiking trip undertaken by him and his friends in 1901. Among these memories lie clues to the location where the party encountered 'the great thrill of our expedition' – a pair of huia. I'm trying to read the article while keeping up with George and Keena, all the while taking in the dramatic scenery of the forest. According to Messenger, his friend was able to imitate the huia's whistle and a pair of birds came 'bounding out of the ferns and supplejacks' and 'regarded us intently, their heads turning from side to side displaying their orange coloured wattles, the birds had no fear of human beings'. At this point in his story I expected Messenger to reach for his gun, but instead he and his friends enjoyed the privilege and thrill of interacting with these 'rare and beautiful birds', which were 'evidently as curious about our movements as we were of theirs'.

As if sensing some imperceptible change in the landscape, George stops, scans our surroundings and announces reverentially: 'This is it, this is huia country.' We stop and rest in the shade at the creek bend above the ravine where, George believes, Messenger encountered the huia in 1901. Pools of golden sunlight stream through the canopy of tree ferns and towering tōtara, contrasting with the darkness cast by these ancient trees. The huia were here, once, their sleek bodies slipping through the shadows. Over there, on that giant rotting stump, they would have hacked and probed with their beak and their bill. That mossy branch is where they would have called and caressed and fanned their white-tipped tail feathers.

George and Keena start back down along the track and I wait, alone. This place is just how I always imagined it. I stand on the edge of the ravine, put my lips together and whistle; 'uia, uia, uia' 'where are you?', 'where are you?' I wait for a reply. But there's nothing, only silence.

CHAPTER SIX

South Island Kōkako

Callaeas cinereus

GONE: 1967

The woman shuffles uncomfortably close, clasps my hand and, staring straight into my eyes, utters four words that I didn't want to hear. Ten minutes ago I'd been sat alone in this windswept bird hide, a wooden shack stuck out on a remote sandy spit facing the Firth of Thames, the wide coastal bay on New Zealand's North Island. To me, an empty bird hide is like a sacred temple. Within its hallowed timber walls I can achieve an almost meditative state as I sit silently observing the natural world undistracted. And inside this particular bird hide, in the January heat of a different hemisphere, watching unfamiliar shorebirds scuttling on the sand, I feel . . . lighter. Everything I know is half a world away.

My isolation has been shattered by the entrance of a talkative couple who aren't so much interested in bird-watching as simply curious as to why someone's built a shed on a beach miles from anywhere. Our initial 'hellos' betray that we are all English and, during the inevitable follow-up questions, it transpires that we live just a few streets apart in the same English village. While this sobering coincidence sinks in, a fourth person enters the hut, nods his greeting and silently asserts his bird-watching credentials by nimbly assembling a telescope and tripod. 'What's your surname?' the couple ask. 'Blencowe', I reply. The silent bird-watcher swings around, 'You're not *Michael* Blencowe are you?' He too is from England, where we've exchanged emails though never met. I nervously glance to the door, half expecting a procession of old acquaintances to file through, filling up the bird hide like the *This Is Your Life* TV studio. The woman shuffles uncomfortably close: 'It's a small world.'

• • •

I had come to New Zealand hoping I'd find evidence of a big world – that vast, lost world of my childhood, where creatures hid undiscovered in vast mountain ranges and dense forests. My journey had been prompted by a tantalising news story. One of the extinct species from the Booth Museum's display case had reportedly been seen hopping around and acting in an altogether un-extinct sort of way. Could this resurrected creature be living proof of the hope I was seeking, that the world was still big enough to hide extinct animals undetected for decades? As the poet Emily Dickinson said: 'Hope is the thing with feathers.' And my hopes were pinned on a bird: the South Island kōkako.

The South Island kōkako was (or possibly is) a chunky, blue-black bird with bright orange circular facial wattles. Like the huia, it's one of the five endemic New Zealand wattlebirds and, also like the huia, it didn't respond too well to the arrival of predatory mammals. In 2019, the University of Otago and the Swedish Museum of Natural History investigated the demise of the huia and South Island kōkako using similar ancient DNA techniques that we have previously seen employed to understand other bird extinctions. They concluded that both the huia and the South Island kōkako had healthy genetic diversity at the time of their extinction, with no signs of the inbreeding associated with small, isolated populations. Their disappearance had been relatively rapid after humans brought plagues of predators to New Zealand and cut down their home.

The South Island kōkako clung to existence in the forested mountains of New Zealand's South Island until its last confirmed sighting near Mount Aspiring in 1967. In 2007, the Bird Threat Ranking Panel of New Zealand's Department of Conservation declared it officially extinct. However, it seems this particular departmental memo never made it through to the South Island kōkako itself. The bird apparently just couldn't stay extinct. People kept reporting brief sightings or snatches of its haunting church organ-like song. After one apparently convincing sighting near Reefton in 2007, the South Island kōkako found its status resurrected from 'extinct' to 'data deficient', an uncertain halfway house between here and the hereafter. This mysterious, elusive bird earned itself the nickname 'the Grey Ghost'.

In 2010, the South Island Kōkako Charitable Trust was established by a group of people eager to prove that this bird doesn't belong in this book. Their supporters have spent countless hours searching, looking, listening and following leads. Regular social media updates show footage of determined men, bearded and camouflaged, wandering around the dense forests of New Zealand looking like mislaid extras from *The Lord of the Rings*, unaware that Peter Jackson has yelled 'cut'. The Trust has also offered a reward: NZ$10,000 for the first confirmation that the South Island kōkako still flies in New Zealand's forests. All they need is an indisputable photo, a convincing video clip or just one grey feather. Since making the offer they have received over 200 eyewitness reports, although the bird has stubbornly remained camera shy.

Sightings often make the headlines. In 2018, Liam Beattie was hiking the Heaphy Track in the north-west of the South Island and spotted a bird he didn't recognise. He didn't think much of it until he entered the remote hikers' bunkhouse on Gouland Downs. There on the wall a Wild West-style reward poster read: 'Wanted (Preferably Alive)'. The South Island kōkako', above a picture of a bird exactly like the one he had just seen outside. A few weeks later I read about this encounter online. 'It had an orange "thingo" under its beak', Liam said, and was 'just chilling out'. 'It seemed pretty relaxed and didn't seem to be in a hurry to go anywhere.'

• • •

I'm always highly cynical when it comes to sightings of extinct animals, especially when people use words like 'thingo' and 'chilling', but, as I read more and more about recent alleged kōkako encounters, I could not reign in my fantasies. What if, instead of just looking at bones and feathers, I was the guy who actually rediscovered an extinct animal? What if this was my destiny? Though I remained sceptical of the kōkako's continued existence I would be more than happy to prove myself wrong, and I'm sure that NZ$10,000 would ease my humiliation. I took a deep breath and clicked 'buy ticket' on the Air New Zealand website.

After a few weeks in New Zealand searching for what remains of the *definitely* extinct moa and huia, I started preparing for my kōkako quest. But first I needed to acquaint myself with my quarry. The South Island kōkako is survived by a close relative restricted to New Zealand's North Island and therefore unsurprisingly named the North Island kōkako. This species was almost wiped out by incessant predation by rats, stoats and possums, but thanks to effective conservation interventions still survives today in predator-free reserves. It is almost identical to its South Island relative except for one significant feature – its wattles are blue, not orange.

To familiarise myself with the appearance and behaviour of a kōkako, I'm going to have to cheat. Since the 1960s, conservation teams at the Pūkaha National Wildlife Centre north-east of Wellington have been hand-rearing thousands of endangered native animals, slowly restocking New Zealand by releasing them into carefully monitored predator-free wildlife reserves. I buy my ticket and hurry past the Kiwi House and Eel Feeding Platform to Aviary Seven, home to the world's only captive kōkako. My eyes excitedly scan the tree in the enclosure but, after 10 minutes, I reluctantly conclude the cage is empty. A sign informs me that, although the South Island kōkako is 'probably extinct', there are now around 2,000 North Island kōkako in the wild, thanks to conservation efforts. The population of Aviary Seven, however, stubbornly remains at zero. Disappointed, I turn to move on, but it's then I notice a movement among the shadows at the back of the cage. Squinting, I lean forward and press my face against the fencing. With a powerful leap, one of the shadows vaults on to a low branch and in four determined bounds swiftly reaches the treetop from where it launches itself at my face, gracefully crashing into the thin curtain of wire mesh that separates us. I am eye to eye with a North Island kōkako.

With our faces pressed together it's hard to take it all in. A kōkako is a rotund bird. Its black eyes are set in a suave bandit's mask, which lends the enigmatic air of Zorro to its appearance – albeit a Zorro who has had a few too many burritos. The legs are surprisingly long and, as it has just demonstrated, are its primary form of locomotion. The small, rounded wings seem almost inadequate for keeping the bird aloft. Under the hooked beak hang the vivid blue wattles, like two discs of squashed Plasticine. For such a striking-looking animal it can certainly lurk inconspicuously in the shadows. But what has drawn this elusive bird so close to me? I can almost feel some special connection, as if the bird is staring into my very soul and has discovered within me some shared quality that . . .

'It's the beard.' A passing member of staff pushing a wheelbarrow of horse manure stops and calls out to me, snapping me out of my moment of wattlebird intimacy. She wanders over and explains that Kahurangi (the name of this female kōkako) was rescued from an abandoned nest in the Hunua Ranges. 'The guy who hand-reared her had a beard and she became imprinted on men with beards. Because of that she doesn't particularly tolerate members of her own species.' I turn back and look at the kōkako. See, there *was* something we had in common after all. I knew it wasn't just the beard. I lean in close to Kahurangi, 'I'm looking for someone just like you', I whisper, 'but in orange, not blue. Wish me luck.'

The following afternoon I'm travelling by ferry across the Cook Strait back to the South Island. I unexpectedly bump into Dr Colin Miskelly from Te Papa. It's a minor coincidence, but a few days later I meet him yet again in a coastal town 160 kilometres (100 miles) away. Then five minutes later I run into an old work colleague from England.

In light of the incident in the bird hide things are starting to feel slightly surreal, as if New Zealand is so empty that various people from my life are having to play recurring roles as extras in my holiday. I'm starting to eye everyone I see with suspicious familiarity. I'm sure the woman selling me blister pads and a water bottle in the camping shop also played the role of 'woman with wheelbarrow' at the kōkako cage. As I travel along the empty roads, the South Island certainly feels deserted. It is an area larger than England, with a population of around 1.2 million compared to England's 56 million. Is this the kōkako's successful hide-and-seek strategy? To hole up on a large but sparsely populated island? For hours I drive past forested mountain valleys, each one a potential kōkako hideaway. I'm starting to realise you could easily overlook a kōkako in those mountain ranges. Hell, you could probably lose a whole family of yetis in there.

I arrive at the trailhead of the Heaphy Track, a 125-kilometre (78-mile) trail which climbs through lush forests and crosses high plateaus of tussock grass before descending to the palm-fringed beaches of the South Island's west coast. The only infrastructure along the route are a series of hikers' bunkhouses and numerous rat and stoat traps used to control the backcountry's unwanted visitors. I'm hoping that hiding somewhere along the trail there's a South Island kōkako with my name on it and I'm determined to find it. Ready or not, here I come.

• • •

My 70-litre backpack is stuffed with enough food, water and sunscreen for four days 'tramping in the bush', but

I've strapped my most essential item, my digital camera, to my hip like some sharp-shooting sheriff. If a kōkako lands in front of me, I'll need to be quick on the draw to get my photo before it reaches for the sky and flies back into oblivion. News arrives that just two days ago a Department of Conservation ranger heard 'repeated kōkako-like flute calls' about a day's walk ahead. I envisage myself as the man in Rudyard Kipling's poem 'The Explorer', searching for 'Something lost behind the Ranges. Lost and waiting for you. Go!' Alone in a vast wilderness I'm eager to experience the freedom, the peace, the solitude.

This is hell. It's 3 a.m. and I'm sharing a cramped wooden bunkhouse in the back of beyond with 13 complete strangers. My foam earplugs are powerless against their raucous snoring. In my bottom bunk I'm a prisoner in my own sleeping bag; all I can do is peer through the zipped opening to where a silver sliver of moonlight illuminates a poster pinned to the wooden wall. It's the exact same poster that Liam Beattie saw after his sighting of a South Island kōkako 'chilling out' just behind this bunkhouse. Its masked face is the last thing I see as I finally slip into sleep and dream of orange wattles.

At first light I emerge from my cocoon, tiptoe past the snoring strangers and burst from the bunkhouse into another sparkling New Zealand morning. Behind the hut lies 'The Enchanted Forest', a fairy-tale woodland of waterfalls and caves where every tree and rock is festooned with soft mosses; I half expect to see a unicorn trotting past. I find a comfortable spot in a glade and sit, soaking up the silence, waiting for my own mythical creature, the Grey Ghost. It's undeniably exhilarating, the feeling that, at any moment, the paths and destinies of a foraging kōkako and a wandering middle-aged Englishman could cross. I fantasise about returning to the Booth Museum, NZ$10,000 in my back pocket, opening that cabinet of extinct animals and reclaiming the kōkako for the land of the living. I'd raise the stuffed specimen above my head like the World Cup as I'm carried, shoulder high, through the cheering crowds along Dyke Road.

After a few hours of kōkako-free bird-watching, I relax my grip on my camera and despondently head back to the bunkhouse for some lunch. And that's when I see it. I freeze. Standing right there in front of me, maybe just 3 metres (10 feet) away, is a bird. A bird that has been extinct for 50 years. And yet, there it stands, next to the bunkhouse's outdoor toilet. It looks up and fixes me with a hard stare. I fumble for my camera, point and press the shutter button just as the toilet door bursts opens and a woman exits, the swinging door almost knocking the bird to the floor. Unruffled, it maintains its mean stare, its apparent contempt for me now shared by a woman who seems rather perturbed that I'm photographing her coming out of a toilet. She glowers at me as she walks past, leaving me alone with this ridiculous, turkey-sized, shimmering blue-and-green flightless bird with a massive bright red beak. This is my underwhelming introduction to the takahē.

In 1847, Walter Mantell sent a package containing over 700 moa bones to his father, Gideon, in England. Gideon Mantell was not an expert in avian bone identification. Unfortunately, he knew a man who was. Mantell passed the moa bones to Richard Owen, who found among them the remains of an altogether different bird. He named it

Notornis mantelli in honour of Gideon's 'intelligent and enterprising son'. It was assumed this bird, like the moa, was long extinct.

Two years later, while working on the South Island, Walter Mantell made another even more sensational discovery, the skin of a recently killed *Notornis* among the leftovers of a meal eaten by a crew of seal hunters. It was proof that *Notornis* was still alive (or at least it had been) and now we had confirmation of how it tasted:'delicious'. This bird had also been on the menu for the Māori, who knew it as moho on the North Island and takahē on the South Island, although it had not been seen since the arrival of the Europeans. More skins of the South Island's takahē were discovered in 1851, 1879 and 1898, this fourth skin being the finest and placed proudly in Otago Museum where I had seen it a few weeks before. Then the takahē trail went cold. In 1919, the museum's takahē specimen fired the imagination of an 11-year-old boy called Geoffrey, who asked his mother what extinct meant. She replied, 'Well, extinct means it's supposed to be dead.' 'Supposed to be dead' wasn't dead enough for young Geoffrey and, on 20 November 1948, after decades of obsessively searching and hoping, Dr Geoffrey Orbell came face to face with a bird that wasn't supposed to be alive. In a remote valley among the South Island's Murchison Mountains he had discovered the first takahē seen in 50 years. I wish I had been there to see the smile on his face. Since then a pioneering recovery programme has steadily increased wild takahē populations. A recent re-introduction project here along the Heaphy Track has allowed me to have my first encounter with this miraculous bird. The takahē has inspired me; New

Zealand is due for another resurrection. I haul my backpack onto my shoulders and continue my search for the South Island kōkako.

• • •

Everything about this spectacular landscape is big. The mountains, the wide plateaus, the forests, the sky. I tramp for six hours without seeing another person, watching, listening, hoping. Where the trail descends through a dark, densely wooded gully I pause to watch a rifleman, a tiny mouse-like bird, scurrying along a mossy branch. A shadow swoops through the trees. I raise my binoculars and my heart almost stops as I focus on a dark bird with orange patches on its head. It's a tui, a familiar New Zealand species, but those orange patches shouldn't be there. I finally figure out they are circles of bright orange pollen which have been dusted on the bird as it fed on flax flowers, creating the perfect South Island kōkako costume. I wonder, is this what some of the observers have been seeing? The tui glides away, both of us startled by the sound of movement down in the shaded gully below. I scan among the boulders and I'm surprised to see there's a man down there fighting his way through the ferns. I re-focus my binoculars and realise that I've seen him before. Well, it's New Zealand. That doesn't surprise me.

I've never actually met Derry Kingston but, while researching the Heaphy Track online, you couldn't miss the tales of the 'Kingston Flyer', the local legend who has walked this trail over 400 times since 1972. This time round, he confesses, he's taking one of his secret short cuts.

As the man who's walked the Heaphy Track more than anyone, has he ever encountered a South Island kōkako? 'I thought I heard one once', he tells me, 'I got real excited, but when I got a look at the bird it was a kākā', an endemic parrot. 'They can make all sorts of noises.' 'Twenty years ago I met some people who reckoned they heard one a few valleys over', he continues, indicating to a gap in the canopy through which I can glimpse the forested ridges of the mountain ranges stretching south to the horizon. I voice my doubts that the Grey Ghost still exists, but Derry's keen to remind me that there have been an awful lot of sightings from around here; they can't all be wrong. However, what he does know for sure is that there are plenty of rats and stoats along the trail. 'Stoats are dumb', he says, 'but rats can climb to feed on chicks and eggs. These days some of these rats hardly ever come down to the ground.'

Derry cheerfully wishes me 'good luck' and heads off along the track. Five months from now, while exploring these mountains, he'll lose his footing and fall 30 metres (100 feet) from a cliff edge. Gashed and bruised he'll spend 30 hours passing in and out of consciousness as death and sand flies circle around him. Thankfully he'll be discovered by rescuers and make a full recovery. I guess we never know what's around the corner. But as the end of the trail approaches I know that there isn't a South Island kōkako waiting around mine.

● ● ●

After four days of searching I can at least appreciate how a bird could hide from humans within this vast landscape.

I may not have found fame or fortune, but I did find a lost world of mountains and dark forests. Sadly, other mammals invaded this paradise a long time before me. The South Island kōkako may well have been able to hide from humans, but it surely couldn't have hidden from those multitudes of killers that humans have let loose upon New Zealand since the middle of the nineteenth century – the rats, stoats, cats, possums and other predators that continue to decimate New Zealand's birdlife to this day.

Where the trail meets the west coast I prop my backpack against a sturdy nikau palm, collapse on the warm, soothing sand and listen to the restless roar of the Tasman Sea breaking along miles of empty beach. I've saved a warm bottle of Moa lager just for this moment. While watching the waves, I raise a toast to the conservationists who are fighting to save New Zealand's unique and wonderful birdlife. And to those kōkako hunters, here's to their optimism. I wish I could share their faith that the Grey Ghost is still out there.

It's time for me to head back home. I'm a long way from the Booth Museum. I think of the museum's clock, its hands stuck in time: three minutes to twelve. And inside, in that display cabinet of extinct animals, the South Island kōkako still sits alongside the huia and a moa bone. And that's where it's going to have to stay. I raise my bottle to it, and the other incredible lost birds of New Zealand, take one final swig, grab my backpack and head off along the beach. As I walk along the sandy shoreline the sea rushes up behind me to wash away my footprints. It's as if I had never been there at all.

CHAPTER SEVEN

Xerces Blue

Glaucopsyche xerces

GONE: 1941

From way up here the city looks like a giant movie set. I drop two quarters into the coin slot of a metallic blue telescope and press my eye to the lens. With an unenthusiastic click, the telescope's aperture opens. Panning east to west I half expect to spot Clint Eastwood busting out from Alcatraz or Steve McQueen in his Mustang Fastback screeching around the steep switchback that leads here to the summit of Twin Peaks, my panoramic viewpoint over San Francisco. The iconic landscape of 'The City by the Bay' seems a world apart from the remote islands and dense forests that have provided the backdrop for our previous extinction stories. Yet here in 1941, while *Citizen Kane* played at the Geary theatre, Glen Miller topped the *Billboard* charts and a bustling city of 600,000 people went about their day, another beautiful animal vanished forever. And nobody even noticed it had gone.

I sweep the telescope to the west, scanning over the Sunset District, the colourful blocks of residential houses that lie between me and the Pacific. Somewhere out there, around 1851, a lepidopterist swung his butterfly net and collected the first known specimens of a metallic blue butterfly. Panning back east I can just make out one of the world's most recognisable landmarks, the Golden Gate Bridge, lurking somewhere in the fog behind the grassy hump of the Presidio. It was in this parkland in 1941 that another naturalist would take a similar swipe and net himself a specimen of this beautiful butterfly to add to his collection. It was a flick of the wrist that would haunt him his entire life. He would later lament, 'I could never have imagined it would be the last one seen alive.' Time's up. The telescope's aperture clicks and closes.

As the sun sets over the Pacific, the homes, skyscrapers and streets of the second-most densely populated city in the United States are lighting up. It's hard to imagine a time when this landscape was nothing but hilly grassland and an extensive system of amorphous sand dunes constantly moulded by the winds blowing in from the ocean. Only 175 years ago, the area was home to just a few hundred people living in a small settlement, which, following a victory in the Mexican-American war, changed its name in January 1847; adios Yerba Buena, howdy San Francisco. But there were much bigger changes on the way for this quiet coastal community. A year later, on 24 January 1848, James Marshall noticed something gleaming in the river below his sawmill in the foothills of the Sierra Nevada mountains and plunged his hand into the cold water. And with that simple action, the course of world history changed. While Marshall contemplated the golden nuggets of shining metal in his hand, the pale green caterpillars of an as yet unknown butterfly slept in the sand dunes of San Francisco 177 kilometres (110 miles) to the south-west. Marshall's discovery of gold would inadvertently lead to the discovery of this precious blue butterfly and ultimately hasten its extinction. It would all happen in a rush.

• • •

It must have felt like the entire world had descended on San Francisco. From a population of around 800 in 1848, the settlement exploded into a bustling port of 25,000 by 1849. Gold fever drew people from all corners of the planet to California, and for many San Francisco was their point of entry. The goldfields of the Sierra Nevada swarmed with desperate men hellbent on finding their fortune. Through this volatile landscape of mountains, miners, greed and grizzlies marched a man armed with a butterfly net. Frenchman Pierre Lorquin was a lawyer by profession and an entomologist through passion. California called to him, a promised land where he might find both his fortune and a wealth of undiscovered butterflies. And if he found neither, he could put his legal skills to use resolving those miners' squabbles that weren't settled through the traditional 'pickaxe to the head' approach.

In 1849, California was still a wilderness and its natural history was virtually unknown. Further north along the Pacific coast, Georg Steller had been the first naturalist to visit Alaska a century earlier and, as I drove south along Highway 1 to San Francisco, I was often reminded of Steller's frantic 10-hour visit to America on 20 July 1741. Steller's jay, the bird he discovered that day, swooped across the highway and between the colossal coastal redwoods. Where the highway joined the coast, I watched Steller's sea lions basking on offshore rocks, another species discovered by Steller during his 10 months as a castaway.

● ● ●

Forty-five years after Steller and the crew of the *St Peter* had been unceremoniously dumped on Bering Island, the first naturalists to visit California were making an altogether more dignified arrival in Monterey Bay. This French expedition, on board the elegant frigates *L'Astrolabe* and *La Boussole*, was the idea of Louis XVI. The French king and Marie Antoinette had waved *au revoir* to the intrepid naturalists in 1785 and they set foot in California a year later on 15 September. They were greeted warmly by the Spanish inhabitants and unloaded their scientific surveying equipment. The first butterfly net had arrived in California.

Following this pioneering French visit, a steady stream of naturalists visited California including, in 1837, Captain Belcher aboard the HMS *Sulphur*. Belcher spent a month exploring the rivers and marshes around Yerba Buena, discovering and documenting its landscape, wildlife and tribes. Whether he wielded a butterfly net is unknown, but back on board the *Sulphur* he carried the skin of a spectacled cormorant destined to be cuddled by me in Tring 180 years later.

But for this story we're only interested in one butterfly net, that of Pierre Lorquin, who, we understand, arrived some time during the gold rush in 1849 or 1850. The Californian butterflies Lorquin discovered were netted, killed and dispatched back home to his mentor in Paris, one of the most celebrated lepidopterists in all France, Jean Baptiste Boisduval. Lorquin's adventures in California are not documented in any known journal, but it seems he spent more time twirling his butterfly net than swirling his gold panning tray as he, in Boisduval's words, braved 'the tooth of the grizzly and the fang of the rattlesnake'. While gold-crazed men detonated entire hillsides with dynamite, Lorquin continued to carefully post his fragile parcels of butterflies back to Paris, where Boisduval studied and described each delicate specimen. Among them were some species new to science, including a small, metallic blue butterfly found, according to Lorquin's label, in the '*environs de San Francisco*'. In 1852, the same year that the great auk and spectacled cormorant disappeared forever beneath the waves, Boisduval published a paper in the *Annales de la Société Entomologique de France* that introduced a new animal to the world.

He named the butterfly after Xerxes the Great – the fifth-century ruler of Persia (but with the French spelling Xerces). It was a new addition to the world's second-largest butterfly family, the Lycaenidae: the gossamer-winged butterflies, which include the blues, coppers, hairstreaks, sunbeams and harvesters. With over 6,000 species worldwide, the Lycaenidae form one-third of the estimated 18,500 known butterfly species on Earth.

The Xerces blue was the embodiment of California. Its cerulean wings sparkled like sunlight on the Pacific and it spent its whole life at the beach. It could only have been more Californian if we had taught it to whistle some Beach Boys tunes. The male's blue upperwings were accentuated by a black, then white, fringe. The female, like many females in the 'blue' family, had completely brown upperwings, although at certain angles a twinkle of blue would dance across the wings to remind you where her allegiances lay. Boisduval described the undersides of the wings of both sexes as 'dark grey, with a central spot and an interrupted sinuous band, formed of large white dots'. Some individuals differed by having black 'pupils' in these dots and this variant form was named *polyphemus* after a savage one-eyed giant of Greek mythology.

The butterfly burst from its pupa and flew in March and April. Males and females met and mated among the dunes and laid their eggs. Like all butterflies, their caterpillars were fussy eaters and were only able to digest leaves from specific plants. In the case of the Xerces blue, the caterpillars mainly fed on lupins and deerweed – native plants that can tolerate the well-drained soils of a sand dune system. Like Persian King Xerxes himself, the Xerces blue held command over an empire of sand.

● ● ●

The desolate landscape of shape-shifting sand dunes that dominated the Pacific side of the San Francisco peninsula was known by locals as the 'Outside Lands'. In the first few decades of the 1900s, lepidopterists would pack their butterfly nets and take the streetcar to the end of the line at 19th Avenue; from here they would disembark and continue west over almost 3 kilometres (2 miles) of dunes before reaching the sea and not see another soul all day. I'm imagining this barren wilderness as I watch 19th Avenue flash past the bus window and we continue rattling west past 20th Avenue, 21st Avenue, 22nd Avenue . . . and 24 more blocks of houses, restaurants and stores that were built upon the home of the Xerces blue. Witnessing this development, local entomologist Hans Hermann Behr wrote of the butterfly, 'The locality where it used to be found is converted into building lots, and between German chickens and Irish hogs no insect can exist besides louse and flea.' The bus comes to a stop just after 48th Avenue and the driver leans out of his cab and announces 'End of the line, Ocean Beach' to the only passenger left on the bus. I clamber off. Westward from here there's a highway, a strip of beach and then the Pacific. There is nothing left of the Xerces blue's empire.

I spend some time wandering around these streets and stop in at a local deli to pick up something for lunch. From behind the counter the cheery owner, who is preparing my mortadella on sourdough sandwich, informs me that once a month his deli doubles as the headquarters for the Golden Gate chapter of Starfleet, The International Star Trek Fan Association. With his breadknife he proudly indicates a framed poster signed by his hero William Shatner, Captain James T. Kirk himself, a man whose intergalactic mission was to 'seek out new life'. As I pay for my lunch I wonder if he is aware that here, where California meets the Pacific on the final frontier of the American West, a small, blue life form from his home planet had been wiped out to build this neighbourhood.

With fog rolling in from the Pacific I walk along the Great Highway, up over the headland and hike alongside the waters of the Golden Gate. After an hour, I find a bench, reach in my backpack and find my mortadella sandwich, although I seem to have misplaced the Golden Gate Bridge. It's hiding somewhere in front of me, and momentarily drifts out of the fog and into focus. I plug in my headphones. On the San Francisco playlist I have compiled, I skip past the Grateful Dead and the Dead Kennedys to Bay Area folk band The Frail Ophelias and their song 'Xerces Blue'. Over the lonely twang of a banjo, the singer's voice serenades the 'lavender blue and white' butterfly 'falling, never to rise again' while the Golden Gate Bridge coyly reveals more of itself to me. In May 1937, hundreds of thousands of smiling people walked, drove, cycled and roller-skated across the bridge as part of its opening ceremonies. Not one of them aware that just over a mile away the unchecked growth of

San Francisco was killing something that, while infinitely smaller than this landmark, was just as unique to their city. I can't blame them for their ignorance. At the time even the local entomologists who studied this butterfly were largely unaware too. Scientists and collectors kept on taking specimens of the Xerces blue and, as numbers declined, they comforted themselves in the knowledge that there must be other populations somewhere else on the sand dunes. But these assumed 'somewhere elses' were getting fewer and farther between. As San Francisco expanded, the sands and time were running out for the Xerces blue.

● ● ●

From my bench it's a short stroll down to the Presidio, a former military fort, which for decades has served as a vital green space for the city's swelling population. Here, at the start of the 1940s, among the dwindling dunes of Lobos Creek, a patch of deerweed just 21 metres (68 feet) wide by 46 metres (150 feet) long represented the worldwide distribution of the Xerces blue. It was here, in the spring of 1941, that William 'Harry' Lange captured a Xerces blue in his butterfly net. Unaware of the tragic significance of what he was doing, he transferred it to his killing jar. As the chemical fumes inside the glass container slowly suffocated the last known individual of this species, its beating blue wings slowed and stilled. The butterfly was added to Lange's reference collection, an entomological pin thrust through its thorax. The final nail in the coffin of the Xerces blue.

Despite a distinguished career as professor of entomology at the University of California, Harry would forever be known as the man who unknowingly killed the last known Xerces blue. In 1998, at the age of 86, he was still being asked about that day. Standing in Lobos Creek, on what was now a parking lot, Harry was interviewed for an article for the National Wildlife Foundation. 'There were no real surveys of the Xerces at the time and we had no idea it was close to extinction', Harry recalled, then added, 'I always thought there would be more. I was wrong.' But Harry is not the villain in this story; he was just the final witness to the extinction of a species. It wasn't an oblivious entomologist but the decades of relentless destruction of the butterfly's sand dunes for urban development that had wiped it out. San Francisco had killed the Xerces blue.

• • •

In a subterranean, climate-controlled vault, a glass-topped drawer labelled '*Glaucopsyche xerces*' slides out of a metal cabinet and is placed in front of me. The precious contents within are ordered in serried rows like a jeweller's display case. Over 100 butterflies are posed on pins, displaying their blue or brown upper sides or their pale freckled undersides. Some of the specimens look so perfect, so pristine, every scale, every hair still intact. There's only one thing missing from their fragile bodies: life. As the drawer is carefully placed in front of me, the overhead lights reflect across every individual scale on each wing and a shimmering wave of life ripples across their ranks, momentarily re-animating the glittering ghosts of the last legions of the Xerces blues. It's that same illusion of life I've seen shimmering across the iridescent feathers of the spectacled cormorant and the huia.

Each butterfly is pinned above a handwritten label, a gravestone of sorts, denoting the date and the location within San Francisco where the butterfly was caught and killed: 1932, 1937, 1938; Lake Merced, The Presidio, Twin Peaks. The final inscribed detail is the name of the obsessive collector or oblivious entomologist who took it. There, at the back, I can see Harry Lange's specimen dated 23 March 1941 – one of the final Xerces blues collected from Lobos Creek, just a 45-minute walk from this basement storeroom in the California Academy of Sciences.

The California Academy of Sciences is housed inside an impressive eco-friendly building on Music Concourse Drive in Golden Gate Park. The lush 4-square-kilometre (1000-acre) park itself was established over the barren sand dunes of the 'Outside Lands'. These days the nearest thing to Xerces blue habitat you'll find here are the bunkers of the park's golf course. The Academy was founded in 1853 and, like Captain Kirk, they too are on a mission: 'To explore, explain, and sustain life.' It's a task they're achieving admirably from their Golden Gate Park headquarters. Here you'll find a planetarium, aquarium, mini-rainforest and museum all under one (green) roof. Among its 46 million scientific specimens, the Academy is the custodian of the largest collection of Xerces blue butterflies in the world.

David Bettman, a curatorial assistant in the entomology department of the California Academy of Sciences, gazes at the pinned specimens with a familiar expression, one which I've seen on the faces of all the curators I've met on my journey – somewhere between wonder and regret. David is a passionate entomologist with a particular interest in butterflies. He shares his knowledge of the Xerces blue as I run through the list of questions in my notebook. As a keen amateur entomologist myself, David has perceived in me a kindred spirit. 'It is frustrating how extinct insects are always overlooked in favour of extinct birds and mammals, the big, showy stuff, isn't it?' David says. 'Oh, definitely', I smile and nod, but even as those words are leaving my lips it dawns on me. While I know the details of dozens of extinct birds and mammals – 'the big, showy stuff' – I can only name one extinct insect: the Xerces blue.

● ● ●

David slides a new drawer labelled 'Extinct Insects' on to the worktop. 'Well, I'm sure you'll be interested in seeing these then', David says as he gestures towards what look like three particularly parched cigars, 'We're really lucky to have them.' My vacant stare is conveying to David that he may have misjudged me and I'm actually more of a 'big and showy' kind of guy after all. 'You must have heard of the Rocky Mountain locust?' he asks incredulously. I'm about to find out that claiming to be an entomologist interested in extinct animals and not knowing about the Rocky Mountain locust is like claiming to be a meteorologist and never having heard of the rain.

The Rocky Mountain locust was more of a force of nature than an insect. Individuals formed swarms over the western United States so large you could measure them in countries. It is claimed one swarm in 1875 was the size of Spain (or two New Zealands). Some estimate it contained 12.5 trillion locusts, the greatest concentration of animals ever recorded on Earth. But by 1902 the locusts were gone and only a few examples remain in museums, the scarcity of specimens almost as unbelievable as the size of their immense swarms. Then again, if you were faced with 12.5 trillion of anything, grabbing a few 'just in case they run out' would be the last thing on your mind. The desiccated trio in the drawer now lie like entombed pharaohs, all that remains of an ancient civilisation. David explains that the mechanism behind their extinction isn't totally certain, although changes in agricultural practices caused by the arrival of frontier farmers may have interrupted their life cycle. We're joined by Chris Grinter, collections manager of entomology, who until now has been enthusiastically converting a group of schoolchildren into future naturalists by showing them some of the incredible beetles in the Academy's collections. David and Chris spend time telling me the histories of the other unfortunate inhabitants of the 'Extinct Insects' drawer before packing them away.

I ask, 'Are there any other specimens that the Academy is particularly noted for?' Chris and David exchange glances, then Chris looks back at me, 'You do know about our tortoises, don't you?' My blank expression yet again betrays that I haven't done my homework. 'Tortoises? What tortoises?'

CHAPTER EIGHT

Pinta Island Tortoise

Chelonoidis abingdonii

GONE: 24 June 2012

A solemn, suited doorman guards the building's grand archway. On the sidewalk a man steadies his selfie stick and huddles his wife and young daughters closer, waving and grinning for a family photo. Their laughter strikes me as rather disrespectful considering they're visiting the location where a man was shot and killed. Standing on the corner of West 72nd Street I watch them from somewhere between despair and disbelief. To them it's just another tourist attraction, another picture for their Instagram page: #newyork #imagine #johnlennon.

I can still remember getting ready for school and hearing on the radio that one of The Beatles had been murdered. On 8 December 1980, John Lennon was just one individual lost from the 4.5 billion *Homo sapiens* on our planet. Some members of our species rise to such prominence that the entire world seems to stand still and mourn their passing, yet we rarely have the opportunity to collectively mourn the moment an entire species is lost.

●　●　●

On 24 June 2012, I came home from work and read the news that a species had become extinct. The last surviving Pinta Island tortoise had been discovered dead on the floor of his pen by his keeper. Conservationists had desperately searched for others of his kind in the hope that, through breeding, they could prevent this fateful day. For four decades the tortoise waited. He never found a partner, but he found international fame as a symbol of hope through conservation and, as the only living member of his species, he gained the world's sympathy. Because no matter how lonely you feel, you'll never be as alone as Lonesome George.

Tortoises have always had a special place in my heart. When I was three years old my parents presented me with a pet tortoise, which I named Tootles. I suppose that a pet can offer a child affectionate interaction and, upon its death, can teach a lesson in mortality. Tootles is neither affectionate nor dead. For the past 48 years he has ignored me while he slowly stomps around the garden on his little leathery legs.

No one was exactly sure of Lonesome George's age when he died, although the consensus seems to be that he was just over 100 years old. Giant tortoises are among the world's longest-lived animals – the current record holder, Jonathan, hatched in 1832, the same year that Georges Cuvier died and Lewis Carroll was born, and is still going strong at 188. So, Lonesome George's death came as a shock to everyone, his passing hitting the world's headlines and generating a global tsunami of sadness. It was decided that, in order to preserve George's conservation message, George himself had to be preserved and displayed, so his 75-kilogram (165-pound) body was quickly mummified in plastic and transferred to a freezer. A crate was constructed, permits were obtained and his body was flown to a workshop just off Christopher Columbus Highway in New Jersey. Here George Dante, one of the best taxidermists in the business, got to work. Lonesome George was defrosted, moulded, skinned, sculpted, painted and polished. After a year of painstaking, respectful and tender craftmanship, the last Pinta Island tortoise was ready to be unveiled and return home, but it would be a long journey. There's not much that's slower than a dead tortoise.

• • •

Pinta Island is the most northerly of the major islands in the Galápagos, the archipelago that lies in the Pacific Ocean 900 kilometres (560 miles) west of Ecuador. Actually, 'lies' isn't the right word; it sounds too restful and the Galápagos are anything but restful. These islands straddle the equator in one of the world's most active volcanic hotspots and are constantly being reborn and remodelled through dramatic eruptions and uplift.

The credit for their discovery goes to the fourth Bishop of Panama whose ship, lost and adrift, landed on these islands on 10 March 1535 and provided us with the islands' first review: 'nothing but seals, turtles and such big tortoises that each could carry a man'. These tortoises were such a striking feature that by the 1570s 'Insulae de los Galopegos' was appearing on maps: The Islands of the Tortoises.

Giant tortoises were once widespread on our planet; these heavily armoured reptiles had conquered every continent except Australia and Antarctica. Now and then tortoises would fall off the continents, but their buoyant bodies – coupled with an ability to survive for months without food and fresh water – allowed them to ride the ocean currents to remote islands. After their extinction on the large landmasses, the only populations that survived into recent history were those established on three island groups: the Seychelles, the Mascarenes (Mauritius, Rodrigues and Réunion) and, the Galápagos.

On 17 September 1835, another the Galápagos Islands' most celebrated visitors bobbed ashore in his rowing boat and stepped out onto the bleak, black basalt.

Charles Darwin's initial opinions of the islands were never destined to be adopted as slogans by the Galápagos tourist board: 'Nothing can be imagined more rough or horrid', 'Reminds me of Wolverhampton'. To Darwin, the steaming craters and cones were as picturesque as the slagheaps and spoils of England's industrial wastelands. He would spend five weeks here collecting specimens of plants ('wretched looking little weeds') and animals. Darwin seemed to take a particular dislike to the marine iguanas ('disgusting, clumsy lizards' with a 'hideous head') which sat soaking up the sun on the shore. He flung one into the sea by its tail just to see what would happen. It turns out they faithfully struggle back to their original sunbathing spot. So, Darwin flung it back into the sea again. Several times.

But there was no way Darwin was tossing a giant tortoise in the Pacific: 'They were so heavy', he wrote, 'I could scarcely lift them off the ground.' He marvelled at these prehistoric-looking creatures as they marched around him, hissing their contempt if he came too close. Darwin noted how their low, lumbering bodies had carved ancient highways that radiated out across the barren landscape from the precious pools of fresh water. Here he stood, amused, as they'd arrive, plunge their heads in the water and 'swallow about 10 mouthfuls a minute'. Darwin just couldn't resist hopping on their backs – 'after a few raps on the hinder part of their shells, they would rise up and walk away', although he didn't master the skill of maintaining his balance for long.

When he wasn't playing iguana boomerang or riding in a reptile rodeo, Darwin found time to dine with the Norwegian-born vice-governor of Floreana Island,

Nicholas Lawson, who told tales of tortoises so large they required 'six or eight men to lift them from the ground'. Lawson also mentioned to Darwin that he could tell which island a tortoise came from by the shape of its shell. Darwin later admitted that he should have paid more attention to this comment, but he had other things on his mind. During Darwin's time on the Galápagos an idea was forming somewhere in his brain. A very big idea. So, let's leave Darwin riding into the sunset astride a giant tortoise, searching for that clue which could help him unravel the greatest of life's mysteries, blissfully unaware that he is sat on it.

Nicholas Lawson had been right. The tortoises found on different islands in the Galápagos were indeed different. An example of evolution in action, the tortoises had diversified into 15 separate species adapted to the different habitats of each island. Separate species could be identified by subtle differences in their carapace characteristics. Broadly speaking, on the more arid islands the tortoises are smaller with 'saddleback' shells that have a rising rim along the front edge. This rim allows them to stretch their necks up to feed on taller vegetation and to hold their heads high in displays of dominance. On humid islands blessed with lush, low-growing vegetation the tortoises kept their heads down. These species' shells are domed, with no need for the rising rim. Nicholas Lawson may have been right about the variety of tortoises, but he was wrong about one thing. During his dinner with Darwin in 1835 he predicted that the giant tortoises of Floreana Island would be extinct in 20 years. They were extinct in 10 years.

• • •

Not once in the past 48 years have I looked at Tootles' wrinkled neck and scaly legs and thought that he looked tasty; yet, according to one early Galápagos visitor, tortoises were 'considered by all as the most delicious food we had ever tasted'. Tortoises became the perfect takeaway meal. They came in their own packaging and could be conveniently stacked upside down and stored in the ship's hold. They didn't require water or food and stayed alive and fresh for months until you were ready to pop one in the pot. Since the discovery of the islands, everyone from pirates and whalers to British naval officers and California-bound gold-diggers would swing by and stock up on Galápagos tortoises. Smaller female tortoises were more regularly taken; they were lighter to carry and, as they laid their eggs in soft sand, tended to be found closer to the ships. Onshore, the Galápagos islanders casually killed tortoises for food, took a handful of meat for their meal and left the rest for the introduced rats and dogs, which also dug up eggs or devoured the young tortoises as they emerged. Gangs of men scoured each island, methodically massacring every tortoise and scraping out the fat stored under their shells. Melted down, this fat made a clear, valuable oil, which was burned to light the streetlamps of Ecuador. It has been estimated that up to 200,000 tortoises were slaughtered before the twentieth century.

In 1891, German paleontologist Georg Baur visited the Galápagos and witnessed the tortoises, the living evidence of evolution, being destroyed and lost to science. He sent up a distress flare to the world's zoologists urging that these vanishing animals should be collected 'before it is too late. I repeat, *before it is too late!*'

• • •

Walter Rothschild, the world's greatest collector of natural history, was the man to answer Baur's plea. Rothschild naturally desired a specimen of each Galápagos tortoise species for his collection. But giant tortoises were more than just ticks on a checklist to Rothschild; he had a genuine love for these animals and was passionate about their conservation. When Rothschild heard that the tortoises of Pinzón, a small island in the centre of the Galápagos, were destined to be eaten into extinction within two or three years, he funded a salvage mission to the archipelago to bring back every tortoise that could be found, 'large or small, dead or alive'. This 1897 expedition spent three and a half months in the Galápagos, returning with 60 crates of specimens and 65 tortoises for Rothschild. They also brought back horror stories of the tortoise massacre they had witnessed. Rothschild predicted in 1898 that in three years there would not be a living giant tortoise of any kind on the Galápagos Islands. In 1900, he would come to the aid of the Aldabra giant tortoise of the Seychelles by dipping into his fortune and leasing their Indian Ocean island home, making remote Aldabra Atoll part of his private estate. In 1901, Rothschild sent Californian collector Rollo Beck on another Galápagos mission.

Beck had been part of the 1897 expedition and had proved himself to be single-minded and selfless in the pursuit of a specimen. At the top of Rothschild's 1901 wish list was a species that had been missed in 1897 and therefore highly coveted for his collection: the Pinta Island tortoise. This time Beck proved his diligence, locating two tortoises on Pinta. The first, an old male that Beck dubbed 'Old Mossback', was too big to carry over Pinta's challenging volcanic terrain, so it was killed and skinned in situ. The second tortoise had seemingly become trapped after falling from a cliff and had lost an eye. Its smaller, simpler shell indicated that this was a female and, if so, would be the only known female Pinta Island tortoise. Beck was keen to transport her to England alive but suspected that she would not survive the trip, and so this one-eyed lady was killed, skinned and prepared.

Photos taken by Beck during the 1901 expedition contain unbearable images of utter devastation and carnage. The watering holes where Darwin observed tortoises drinking were now graveyards. Smashed fragments of tortoise carapace stretched to the horizon, the desolate landscape resembling a tabletop littered with shattered walnut shells. These sickening images are hard to look at. It isn't much easier reading the accounts of the naturalists who captured and killed tortoises in the name of science, prompted by the relentless massacre on the Galápagos that legitimised their actions at the time. This was what conservation looked like at the start of the twentieth century – a race not to save species but to save specimens before they were lost to science.

● ● ●

On the morning of 28 June 1905, a tugboat led a schooner of 11 sailors and scientists west through San Francisco's foggy

Golden Gate, the same short journey made by Leonhard Stejneger 23 years earlier. Upon reaching the Pacific where Stejneger's steamer had turned north, the schooner raised its sails and headed south, Galápagos bound, on a 17-month collecting expedition led by Rollo Beck under orders from the California Academy of Sciences.

Nine months later, on 4 April 1906, after relentlessly collecting thousands of specimens throughout the Galápagos, we find Beck alone in the moonlight on the coal black volcano of one of the archipelago's least explored islands: Fernandina. Exhausted after three days hiking and hunting, Beck sits enjoying his supper of tinned fish and coffee while keeping a watchful eye on his momentous discovery – the large male tortoise grazing alongside him. Beck knew this was the first tortoise that had ever been reported from this island. He did not know it would also be the last. It would be far too heavy to carry back over the treacherous terrain to the schooner, so Rollo Beck finished his coffee, reached for his knife and sent the Fernandina Island tortoise into extinction. A fortnight later Earth also demonstrated its capacity for obliteration.

● ● ●

At 5:12 a.m. on Wednesday, 18 April 1906, the most destructive earthquake in the history of the United States struck San Francisco; the tremors and resultant fires destroying 80 per cent of the city. The California Academy of Science's museum on Market Street was partially destroyed and, as the inferno approached, the staff rallied to save what they could. Botanist Alice Eastwood gallantly climbed the crumbling staircase and lowered valuable specimens from the balconies on a rope made from strips of her undergarments. Tens of thousands of specimens were lost, among them Xerces blues collected by Lorquin and, according to Stejneger, the world's finest skeleton of Steller's sea cow. In the Galápagos, the scientists heard of the devastation in San Francisco and realised the importance of the specimens in their ship's hold: 'We are the academy now.'

Ten years later, the California Academy of Sciences relocated to its present site in Golden Gate Park. Following another earthquake in 1989, the building was redesigned and rebuilt 'to withstand whatever San Francisco can throw at us', says collections manager of entomology, Chris Grinter. He and curatorial assistant David Bettman, have returned the extinct insects to their secure cabinet and have led me down to a reinforced door deep in the building's basement. 'When Rollo Beck's expedition returned to what remained of San Francisco in 1906, they brought back the collection which rebuilt the Academy', Chris tells me. 'Seventy-eight thousand specimens including . . . ' he presses his security laminate to the reader, pausing as a light changes from red to green ' . . . 266 tortoises.' The heavy door opens, we step into a large, cold bunker and stand among a herd of Galápagos giant tortoises. While 130 Xerces blues fit neatly in one drawer, storing hundreds of Galápagos tortoises is a major undertaking. They are mostly skinned specimens shrouded in polythene, although a stuffed and mounted pair, their wrinkled necks outstretched, scowl at us from a top shelf like two elderly sentries. Chris turns to me, 'I have to warn you, they've all be arsenated.' My face conveys my concern as to what this intrusive-sounding procedure had entailed. Chris clarifies, 'Treated with arsenic. So, don't lick them.' Up until that point I had no intention of licking a giant tortoise, but you know how when someone tells you not to do something you immediately want to do it?

Each tortoise's tag contains important details of its island of origin and we locate one of the three male specimens killed and collected from Pinta Island in 1906. I wonder if it could be a close relation to Lonesome George, Old Mossback or the one-eyed lady. Standing here among these lifeless shells, Chris, David and I reflect on how attitudes and options have improved in just over a century. Today, the California Academy of Sciences undertakes ambitious global conservation and restoration projects while on the Galápagos, pioneering conservation initiatives and enforced legal protections are overseen by the Galápagos Conservancy and the Galápagos National Park Directorate. We've come a long way.

Along an aisle lined with domed shells, one tortoise defiantly sticks his neck out. Chris introduces him: 'And this is *Chelonoidis phantastica,* the Fernandina Island tortoise.' This is the male saddleback skinned by Rollo Beck in the moonlight on 4 April 1906. 'He's the only known specimen of this species in the world, dead or alive.' As Chris spoke, it may just have been my imagination or perhaps the flickering storeroom lights reflected in its glassy eyes, but I could have sworn this tortoise just winked at me.

For decades, the Academy's three specimens of the Pinta Island tortoise represented the last known sightings of this species. It is unknown how many more tortoises were collected from Pinta after 1906, whether in the name of science or in the name of supper. We do know that sometime around 1959 three goats were released on Pinta by fishermen hoping to establish a food supply for future visits. The goats multiplied, munching on the island's vegetation, changing the landscape and decimating the food available to any remaining Pinta Island tortoises. Wardens would eventually eradicate the herds, shooting 40,000 goats in 20 years.

● ● ●

On 1 December 1971, Hungarian scientist József Vágvölgyi and his wife were rare visitors on Pinta and, while studying snails, bumped into a rare resident: a large male tortoise. After a few contemptuous hisses, it smiled for their camera. The Vágvölgyis were unaware of the significance, but their photo was a revelation – the first tortoise reported from Pinta for 65 years. The following spring, this male Pinta Island tortoise was retrieved and brought to live in the safety of the Charles Darwin Research Centre on Santa Cruz Island.

And so began the legend of Lonesome George, the last of his kind. A $10,000 reward was immediately offered for a female Pinta Island tortoise in the hope that one had been captured decades before and was grazing obliviously in a zoo on the other side of the world. Meanwhile, George lived the life of a celebrity. He had a luxury compound with a pool, he put on a lot of weight and the world became unhealthily obsessed with his sex life. Sadly, when he was persuaded to mate with other closely related species the resulting eggs were inviable. Lonesome George even received that highest of celebrity accolades – a death threat. In 1995, local fishermen unhappy with conservation restrictions held the research centre's staff hostage while chanting 'Muerte el Solitario Jorge'. For 40 years, gawking tourists by the thousand queued up to take a picture of the loneliest animal on the planet. And every day George waited to see that glimmer of recognition in the face of another which would let him know he wasn't alone. And then came the morning of 24 June 2012. Lonesome George was found sprawled on the floor of his enclosure by Fausto Llerena, the man who had cared for him for 30 years.

● ● ●

Just a few blocks from the spot where John Lennon fell, Theodore Roosevelt sits astride a bronze horse outside the American Museum of Natural History. I take my place in the queue next to a *Barosaurus*, excited to be fulfilling another childhood dream. I've taken a layover in New York on my journey home to visit this world-famous museum; Lonesome George did the same. On his journey from New Jersey back to the Galápagos, George Dante's magnificent restoration of the world's most famous tortoise was displayed here for four months while visitors filled their Instagram accounts with photos: #newyork #extinction #lonesomegeorge.

I'm four years too late to pay my respects to George, but I still spend hours wandering the museum, wowed by Olmec heads, meteors and mastodons. But what impresses me most are the giant dioramas: widescreen display cases with taxidermy animals recreating epic scenes from around the planet. These dioramas are so immersive that at one point I am literally stunned by them. I was so convinced that I was observing the African savannah that I leant forward and smacked my forehead on the glass so hard and loud that the entire gallery turned and stared and I needed to sit down. These dioramas may be more impressive than those back at the Booth Museum, but the Booth opened in 1874, the same year that the cornerstone of this museum was laid, so, as far as I'm concerned, New York stole the diorama idea from Edward Booth and just supersized them. At least there's less chance of receiving mild concussion at the Booth.

Something that this museum definitely took from England was Walter Rothschild's collection of bird specimens. Behind the semblance of control, the wealthy collector was being blackmailed by a string of mistresses who threatened to bring scandal to the Rothschild family name. To make ends meet he was forced to relinquish his lease on the giant tortoise sanctuary of Aldabra Island and, in 1931, sell almost his entire bird collection to the American Museum of Natural History: 280,000 bird specimens for the bargain price of $225,000. Rothschild sank into depression. Upon his death in 1937 he left his museum and the remainder of his expansive collections to the British Museum. Rothchild's 144 giant tortoise specimens are now scattered throughout the museum storerooms, although I saw Old Mossback, the Pinta Island tortoise collected by Rollo Beck in 1901, on display in Tring. Beck's one-eyed lady, possibly the world's only specimen of a female Pinta Island tortoise, is shut away in storage.

Meanwhile Lonesome George, the loneliest animal in the world, has returned home and stands, head held high, in the Symbol of Hope Exhibition Hall on Santa Cruz Island in the Galápagos. He's not far from the enclosure where he spent the last four decades of his life. Here the information panel on the wall once read: 'Whatever happens to this single animal, let him always remind us that the fate of all living things on Earth is in human hands.'

● ● ●

The morning after I arrived back home in England, I check on Tootles. He's just the same as always – unaffectionate and alive. At least, I presume he's alive. He's hidden deep in his shell, barely breathing, in the middle of his six-month hibernation. I tuck him back in his box and leave him to his tortoise dreams.

Loving a tortoise is a long-term commitment. We've been together nearly 48 years (although he's only been awake for 24 of them). In middle age I still have a childhood pet who, in all probability, will outlive me. I imagine Tootles at my funeral, dressed in black, carrying my coffin to my grave, the bagpiper playing 'Amazing Grace' 127 times until he gets there. Yet Tootles' species is in trouble. *Testudo graeca*, the spur-thighed tortoise, is now classified as vulnerable to extinction. The capture of tortoises to supply the international pet trade has significantly contributed to the decline in wild populations. During breakfast it strikes me that when I excitedly received Tootles as my pet back in the early 1970s I was playing a part in the extinction of a species. As I'm processing this sombre realisation I glance at the headlines and almost choke on my crumpet: 'Extinct Galápagos Tortoise rediscovered after a century'.

Since Rollo Beck had discovered, killed and collected

the world's only known Fernandina Island tortoise, hopeful conservationists have tried in vain to relocate another. Even legendary Himalayan explorer Eric Shipton searched the island in the 1960s, concluding he'd have more chance of finding a yeti than a Fernandina Island tortoise.

Yet, in February 2019, an expedition led by Washington Tapia of the Galápagos Conservancy and Galápagos National Park ranger Jeffreys Málaga crossed Fernandina's immense, black lava fields to a distant patch of green where they discovered an almost mythical creature nonchalantly chowing down on some cactus. 'The emotion was indescribable', said Tapia, 'this was the first tortoise found on Fernandina in more than 100 years!' Just one week earlier I'd been in a cold bunker staring into the glass eyes of the only tortoise ever found on the island and now here was another, its bewildered face plastered across the world's news. Incredibly, this elderly female was estimated to be over 120 years old, meaning Rollo Beck could have walked past her unaware in 1906. It's a good thing that he did.

But is she a pure-bred Fernandina Island tortoise or another Galápagos species that at some point in the last century floated from a neighbouring island across to Fernandina? In 2020, Yale University scientists were analysing her blood samples, while on the Galápagos more expeditions to Fernandina were being planned. Is she a different species? Are there any more on the island? Or have we found ourselves a new contender to move into Lonesome George's enclosure, an heir to his title: the loneliest animal on the planet.

CHAPTER NINE

Dodo

Raphus cucullatus

GONE: *c.* 1680

This level of idolatry is usually reserved for Elvis or Jesus. Every wall is covered in framed dodo artwork: portraits, cartoons, watercolours, kids' scribblings. Dodos carved from wood, sculpted in clay or moulded in papier-mâché cluster in every corner. Books about dodos, scientific monographs and fairy tales fill the shelves. Intricate ceramic dodos line up in display cabinets alongside dodo thimbles, bookmarks, eggcups and matchboxes. There are dodo postcards, corkscrews and keyrings. Dodo plates, playing cards, fridge magnets, bottle openers, badges and stamps. Overwhelmed, I slump onto the soft sofa, sinking amid its embroidered dodo cushions. A man in a dodo T-shirt reaches out and rescues me with a strong cup of tea. In a dodo mug.

● ● ●

The town of Battle sits in the wooded weald of Sussex about an hour's drive from my home. The main attraction for most visitors is Battle Abbey, apparently founded by William the Conqueror in atonement for the blood spilled here on 14 October 1066 – the Battle of Hastings. On the outskirts of the town, on what was the northern edge of the battlefield, one man's bungalow has become a shrine commemorating the victims of another defeat, one which happened around 350 years ago on battlefields 9,600 kilometres (6,000 miles) away.

Ralfe Whistler is an obsessive collector of all things dodo. I had assumed that even Ralfe's name had been taken from *Raphus cucullatus*, but he assures me that this was just a fortunate coincidence. Now in his late 80s, Ralfe has spent decades filling the walls, shelves and cabinets of his home

– 'The Dodo House' – with everything dodo. He proudly introduces me to the inspiration for this fantastic cluttered collection, the seven dodo bones handed down to him by his ornithologist father, fragments of the bird that inspired all of this paraphernalia.

After a second cup of tea I excuse myself to visit the bathroom. Dodos still cover every wall, but something here doesn't feel right: the toilet. The porcelain and plastic seem too pristine, too . . . dodo-less. With nervous trepidation I lift the toilet lid. Surely there isn't? Yep, there it is, on the underside, a red silhouette of a laughing dodo. To be honest if it hadn't been there I'd have been disappointed.

The dodo is an enigma. To be as dead as one is the final word in finality. Yet the dodo has transcended death, becoming caricatured, objectified, merchandised and resurrected as an unlikely and somewhat dumpy messiah. The dodo is one of the most recognisable species that has ever lived. It has achieved a dubious immortality: the smiling face of extinction. The dodo under the toilet lid laughs, I pull the flush and the water swirls round the bowl.

● ● ●

The black sea swirled around the bow as the storm raged, whipping the waves into towering peaks. The entire fleet, eight ships, were at its mercy. They had made steady progress since leaving the Netherlands 100 days earlier but, after rounding the Cape of Good Hope, it must have felt as though God had abandoned them. In the storm, the fleet had become separated and as the tempest subsided, Vice Admiral Wybrant van Warwijck found himself in command of five stray ships and continued sailing east while supplies of water and food dwindled. Forty days later, on 17 September 1598, any lost faith was restored as the Dutch sailors were delivered into paradise. A heavenly vision of rugged mountains and dense forests rose from the ocean before them. Although known to Arab traders and Portuguese explorers, this volcanic island in the middle of the Indian Ocean, 800 kilometres (500 miles) east of Madagascar, had remained uninhabited. The relieved crews found a safe harbour, landed upon the palm-fringed beaches and eagerly stocked up on fresh water and food. There were doves and parrots, fat, tasty and so tame that you could knock them from the trees with a stick. Fish in such abundance that just two men caught enough to feed the crew of the five ships. Tortoises so large that 10 men, so they claimed, could sit and dine inside one of their upturned shells. And . . . What. On. Earth. Is. That?

In the shadows of the ebony trees the sailors encountered birds 'as big as our swans with large heads and on the head a veil as though they had a small hood'. Fearless and flightless, the birds had 'no wings but in their place three or four black quills, and where there should be a tail there are four or five small curled plumes of a greyish colour'. The sailors had never seen anything like them before. The birds were similarly bemused. With no grasp of global commerce, they did not understand that they were witnessing the birth of modern capitalism. The fleet moored in the bay were part of the first attempts by the Dutch to infiltrate the Indonesian spice trade, an expedition that would lead to the formation of the all-powerful international trading conglomerate, the Dutch East India Company.

Vice Admiral van Warwijck claimed the island for the Netherlands and gave it a name: Mauritius. The birds would gain many names too, including *Walckvogel* and *Dronte,* but *Dod-aars*, referring to their fat, tufted behinds, would give rise to the name dodo. There are surprisingly few detailed observations on the dodo's ecology or behaviour – where's a Georg Steller when you need one? From various journals and diaries we glean that dodos apparently ate fruit, made a noise like a gosling and laid a single egg on a nest of grass. They were 'jaunty and audacious of gait' and would use their preposterous hooked beak to defend themselves. These bizarre-looking birds possessed some currency as curiosities. There is evidence of two dodos in the menagerie of the Mogul Emperor Jahangir in Surat, India sometime between 1628 and 1634, and another dodo made it to Nagasaki, Japan in 1647. But there is one part of the dodo legend that, as a child, I found surreal and unimaginably exciting. I still do. There were once dodos in England.

● ● ●

Halfway across Vauxhall Bridge, I pause and look over the red steel railings. Each time I visit London and cross the Thames I inevitably start humming 'Waterloo Sunset' by The Kinks and today is no exception. I watch a cormorant surface briefly in that dirty old river, diving again when it realises it is in the path of a cruise boat crammed with camera-toting tourists. Over the centuries the Thames has bought many visitors to London, but there is one stranger I wish I could have welcomed. Each time I walk around the capital I imagine its streets around 1638: narrow, crowded and dirty. I daydream of a dark doorway and, unfurled outside, a large cloth painted with the image of the bizarre bird on display inside; just pay a few coins at the door and step right up. This is the extraordinary true story of the curiously named Sir Hamon L'Estrange who, intrigued by the painting of this 'strange looking fowle', entered the sideshow with his companions. Inside they encountered a bird being kept in a chamber, dun brown in colour, larger than the biggest turkey 'but stouter and thicker and of a more erect shape'. 'The keeper called it a dodo', L'Estrange recalled, and, if being shown a dodo wasn't remarkable enough, its owner then proceeded to demonstrate the bird's party trick. Taking pebbles ('some as big as nutmegs') from a pile, he fed them to the dodo explaining that they were 'conducing to digestion'.

I have a feeling these spicy peri-peri chicken wings aren't conducive to my digestion. I'm perched on a wall on Tradescant Road, a residential street in the south London borough of Lambeth, enthusiastically tucking into some fast food from the takeaway on the corner. In the early 1600s, Mauritius became a crucial refuelling station for the Dutch East India Company on the arduous trade routes from Europe to the East Indies. Dodos were a local speciality but, although easy to catch, reviews were mixed – somewhere between nauseating and excellent. Dodo hunting, however, would have had a limited impact on the bird's population. There were just never that many people on Mauritius throughout the seventeenth century.

Over millions of years, the dodo's pristine island home had developed its own fragile ecosystem inhabited with a suite of unique species. There were no mammals on

Mauritius so, in the absence of these predators, the dodo had dispensed with flight and adapted to life on the forest floor. Although perfectly suited to island life, it now found itself spectacularly unprepared to face the multitude of mammals that trotted off the visiting ships year upon year. Rats, inadvertently introduced, would have preyed on dodo chicks and competed for the dodo's fallen fruit food. Monkeys, goats, deer and dogs would have had a similar ruinous impact. Pigs were routinely released by sailors to breed and provide food for the crew upon their return. It was reported that these pernicious porkers reached plague proportions on Mauritius. Feeding on fruit, dodo eggs and chicks, they must have surely played a major role in the dodo's extinction.

• • •

In the seventeenth century, when Lambeth was just a small village south of the Thames, a grand house and gardens stood right here. John Tradescant (the Elder) and his son John Tradescant (the Younger) were gardeners of great renown. Working for country estates and royalty, they travelled the world, returning with exotic plants and a haul of weird and wonderful souvenirs. They amassed an incredible collection at their Lambeth estate and opened it for all to view – the first public museum in Britain. The Tradescant Ark was filled with exhibits from all corners of the globe. There were bones, beaks, bodies and bits of unfamiliar creatures, from stuffed armadillos to zebra tails. There was Henry VIII's glove, Pocahontas' father's shell-covered cloak, a unicorn horn cup, a Turkish toothbrush and, lying among this tremendous treasure trove, an exhibit listed as a 'Dodar, from the Island Mauritius, it is not able to flie being so big'.

There are no front gardens in the regimented Victorian terraced homes of Tradescant Road. I stop outside number 43, where an exotic palm tree subverts the concrete uniformity; the Tradescant spirit still survives. A dodo's body was here once, but where had it come from? Was it the body of the dodo seen by Hamon L'Estrange? Or were there other London dodos?

Tradescant (the Younger) died in April 1662 and joined his father in an ornate, marble-topped tomb in the nearby churchyard of St Mary-at-Lambeth.

● ● ●

At the exact same time that the Tradescants' tomb was sealed in London, the fate of the dodo was being sealed on the once pristine paradise of Mauritius. In February 1662, a fleet of seven Dutch East India Company ships heading home from Indonesia encountered a violent storm in the Indian Ocean. Three of the fleet were lost without trace while the *Arnhem* was smashed onto a reef north-east of Mauritius. Around 100 men escaped, crammed into a small boat. After a week adrift, talk turned to cannibalism, so the tastier-looking crewmen were no doubt relieved when land was spotted on 20 February. The months that the shipwrecked men spent on Mauritius were later recounted by German castaway Volkert Evertszen. He recalled that dodos were never encountered on the main island, but the birds were discovered, and hunted, on an offshore islet only accessible by wading at low tide.

This 1662 account is accepted by many as the last sightings of the dodo, however, later reports from an escaped slave and a geophysicist suggest that the dodo probably survived into the 1680s.

In March 1683, the same time that the dodo disappeared from Mauritius, it disappeared from Lambeth too. Antiquarian Elias Ashmole was unscrupulous when it came to getting what he wanted. And what he wanted was the Tradescant Ark. Without an heir, Tradescant (the Younger) had apparently gifted the ark to Ashmole, who then struck a deal with the University of Oxford. He would give them his entire collection, now bolstered by the contents of the Tradescant Ark, only if they built a suitably grandiose building to showcase his treasured exhibits. And name it in his honour. So, the Ark and a dead dodo sailed west along the Thames by barge.

● ● ●

It's my first time in Oxford and I'm worried I may not make it out alive. Since leaving the train station I have almost been flattened by six cyclists. I stop staring at my hand-drawn map and start looking both ways when I cross the street, although I can't miss the Ashmolean Museum; with its grand columns it looks like some opulent Roman temple. This edifice to Ashmole and his ego opened in May 1683 and would be the new home for the Tradescant dodo.

Aside from a dodo foot in London (which was subsequently lost) and two skulls (which were still lurking, unidentified, in boxes in other museums), the Ashmolean specimen was all that remained of the dodo of Mauritius. For decades it was prodded and patted by the public, its feathers fading until, in 1755, it faced its greatest threat: stringent bureaucracy. Museum inspectors declared the deteriorating dodo a disgrace and it was tossed on the fire. But, just in time, our hero appeared. A museum assistant, witnessing the dodo ablaze, threw off his glasses, tore his shirt to the navel and, bellowing a thunderous 'Noooooooo!', cartwheeled into the flames, emerging, slightly singed, with the dodo's head and foot clenched between his teeth. Okay, none of that actually happened, although this apocryphal story has passed into dodo folklore. The truth is less dramatic. The museum staff simply salvaged all they deemed worth saving from the tatty bird, and disposed of the rest. At that time nobody realised the importance of this specimen; people were not aware that dodos were extinct. In fact, extinction wasn't even an option yet – Georges Cuvier would not take to the stage in Paris to announce the concept until 41 years later.

● ● ●

By the 1800s, with so little dodo remaining, people started to wonder what sort of animal had it been? An albatross? A vulture? A squat ostrich? A feathered tortoise? Some even questioned whether it had actually existed at all. Then, in 1840, Professor John Theodore Reinhardt, while searching through odds and ends in the Royal Museum in Copenhagen, not only found and identified a dodo skull but went a step further, boldly proclaiming that the dodo was in fact a giant pigeon, an idea that was ridiculed at the time. Curiosity and scientific interest in the dodo began to build with people clamouring to know more about this unlikely bird. In 1865, a schoolteacher on Mauritius struck dodo gold. George Clark's pupils had told him of a local marsh where bones of an extinct giant tortoise had been discovered. Figuring that if one extinct animal had been found there then why not another, Clark set off for the swamp. He was given permission to search by the landowner, who also loaned his farm labourers, ordering them to wade waist deep in the black water, feeling for bones in the marsh mud with their feet – a task probably not on their original job descriptions. To Clark's delight they found a few dodo bones, but in subsequent excavations Clark found more. A lot more. So many bones, in fact, that today almost every dodo bone exhibited around the world – including the bones at the Booth Museum and those in Ralfe's bungalow in Battle – originated in the Mare aux Songes, the dodo graveyard of south-east Mauritius.

These bones proved invaluable to our understanding of the dodo and brought wealth to George Clark. And they were sure to bring fame and glory to the scientist who got their hands on them first and reconstructed the first dodo skeleton. For a moment it looked like that man would be Cambridge University's Alfred Newton, who was eagerly awaiting a shipment of bones from Mauritius. But wait. Did somebody mention fame and glory? With an evil cackle, his cape billowing in the breeze, Richard Owen swooped in and intercepted Newton's shipments of bones. I may have added the cape and cackle for dramatic effect but, through bribery and blackmail, it was Owen who would take the bones and the acclaim as the first man who presented the scientific world with a reconstructed skeleton of a dodo.

After another 10 minutes of dodging cyclists I find myself standing, suitably amazed, in the impressive main court of the Oxford University Museum of Natural History. I'm sure Owen would love to be standing here too, carved in Caen stone and immortalised alongside the giants of science who stand watch on pillars around the perimeter: Galileo, Linnaeus, Newton, Aristotle. Owen would fume to see his rival Darwin standing among them, although Darwin's statue looks a little shady, leaning against his pillar like some street-corner hoodlum who'd knife you for your wallet. I wait in the corner with Hippocrates. I have an appointment with what's left of a bird that has been on a long, strange journey to reach this museum, its final resting place. I have been kindly offered a behind-the-scenes tour by collections manager Eileen Westwig, who possesses the two essential superpowers required for the tour: a passion for zoology and the ability to run marathons. One minute we're stood among schoolchildren in the main hall, the next we're hurtling along subterranean passageways into a fluid store where two Tasmanian tigers float suspended in liquid-filled glass tubes. I try to keep up with Eileen as she explains that the museum was opened in 1860 and, to fill its galleries, it received two collections, one of which comprised the natural history specimens from the Ashmolean. We jump back momentarily through the bustle of the main court before sneaking through another side door and up, up, up into a storeroom where I catch my breath and catch sight of my beloved huia, a pair, of course, collected by Walter Buller. We climb higher into an attic space where, among the taxidermy mammals, Eileen introduces me to Maclear's rat. Endemic to remote Christmas Island in the Indian

Ocean south of Java and extinct since 1903, this species was wiped out by a disease carried by introduced black rats. Just as I start to feel some sympathy for a rat, I'm whisked down to a room of crustaceans. Here, in drawer 71, sit the crabs collected by Darwin during the voyage of the *Beagle*. I visualise these very claws snapping at Darwin's evolutionist fingers as he reached under the rocks. After a short jog to the finish line Eileen announces, 'And in this cupboard are the surviving specimens that came from the Tradescant Ark.'

● ● ●

Eileen clears a worktop and I'm pleased for the chance to let my heartbeat return to somewhere near normal.

As she opens the cupboard's double doors, I glimpse something that starts my heart racing again: a box, a large grey cardboard box. Eileen lists the assorted Tradescant exhibits that fill the shelves, all of which must have looked so alien to visitors to Lambeth in the seventeenth century. 'A stuffed armadillo, an elephant's tail, a warthog's skull . . . ' To be honest there may as well have been the Ark of the Covenant and the Holy Grail stored in there, because I'm not listening. I can't take my eyes off that grey cardboard box on the third shelf. I know what's in there. Eileen finally reaches towards it, 'And in here . . . ', she gently places the rigid grey box on the worktop. This time I don't even attempt to retain an air of professionalism. I'm so excited I just blurt it out, 'I've wanted to see this my whole life.' 'Well, it is kinda special', Eileen admits, 'The only soft tissue remains of a dodo in the entire world.' She lifts the lid. And there it is. The holiest of my holy relics. It's a face I recognise from my childhood, one I have stared at a thousand times in my books but here it is in the flesh. The gnarled, ancient, leathery flesh.

What's left of the dodo rests inside bespoke foam compartments within the box. The right-hand side of the skull still has the skin attached, but long ago the soft tissue on the left-hand side was peeled off. It sits alongside the bare bone – a dodo death mask. There's a surprisingly large bony left foot, fragments of skin from the foot, the sclerotic plates from the eye and a single tiny, spiny feather on a microscope slide. As I gaze at these assorted remnants, the leftovers from a long journey through time and space, I think of all the people who have also stared in wide-eyed wonder at this extraordinary bird: centuries of scientists and museum visitors, Ashmole, the Tradescants, maybe Sir Hamon L'Estrange, seventeenth-century sailors and the man who snatched this dodo from under the ebony trees of Mauritius. The Oxford dodo has had a long, remarkable history, but only recently have we developed the technology that has allowed us to discover more of its hidden secrets.

In 2002, mitochondrial DNA extraction confirmed that the dodo was indeed a giant pigeon, its closest living relative the gorgeous, iridescent Nicobar pigeon of south-east Asia. It is thought the ancestors of the dodo would have flown, island-hopping, across the ocean, eventually landing on the young volcanic island of Mauritius millions of years ago. Here, like the moa, they slowly evolved into large flightless birds perfectly adapted for survival on a predator-free island. Until humans turned up and wiped them out within a century.

In 2018, the dodo head was investigated using advanced CT scanning technology to create a 3D digital replica that could help researchers understand more about the bird's lineage and how it fed. However, this CT scanner, which had previously been used to retrieve forensic evidence for 60 murder trials, stumbled upon another murder mystery and a long-dead, cold-case crime was reopened.

On the image of the scanned head a number of unusual light spots had appeared. Upon further investigation these turned out to be lead pellets, 1 millimetre in diameter, embedded in the skin and skull. The dodo had been shot in the back of the head. This revelation has thrown the origin of the Oxford dodo into question. If this bird had been Hamon L'Estrange's sideshow dodo why would anyone have shot it? Had it escaped and ran rampaging through the streets of London? Or had this bird been shot while on Mauritius? If so, how had it remained preserved on the long sea journey to London?

I take one last long look at the dodo. A few weeks earlier I had sat watching a dodo dancing awkwardly in Brighton city centre. Some poor soul, dressed in a furry, orange dodo costume, was handing out flyers promoting a new local takeaway, part of the global Dodo Pizza franchise. The dodo resurrected again, an absurd creature, a bird too stupid to survive, complicit in its own extinction. By caricaturing the dodo we have distanced ourselves from the crime we committed. But stood here, staring at these pieces of crinkled skin and bare bone, I finally saw the dodo for what it really was. The dodo was a bird, a wonderful bird that lived on an island in the middle of the ocean. And we killed it. Eileen puts the lid back on the grey cardboard box and places it back in the cupboard.

Before leaving the museum I visit the gift shop and

buy a dodo keyring and a cuddly dodo to send to Ralfe for his collection. Standing in line to pay, I look across at the museum's dodo display case where an articulated skeleton and a feathered reconstruction of the bird stand upon pedestals. When this museum opened in 1860, local schoolteacher Charles Dodgson would regularly bring three children, Lorina, Edith and Alice, here to explore. Dodgson would always pause at the museum's dodo exhibit; maybe he felt an affinity to the bird because his stutter made him pronounce his own name 'Do-do-dodgson'. In his imagination and in his writing, under the name Lewis Carroll, he transported young Alice down a rabbit hole and into a Wonderland where the dodo with his walking cane and cuffs was the leader of the chaotic Caucus race. When Alice presses the dodo for a result it thoughtfully announces, 'EVERYBODY has won, and all must have prizes'.

But in evolution, that crazy race for survival which has generated the incredible diversity of life on Earth, not everybody has been a winner. It's time to take one last whirl with the losers.

CHAPTER TEN

Schomburgk's Deer

Rucervus schomburgki

GONE: 1938

A cheery carnival tune chimes as the merry-go-round spins. A laughing girl riding on the carousel waves at her father's camera as she glides past, vanishes and then reappears again, still laughing. I'm sitting on a nearby bench observing this happy scene, eating a chocolate ice cream and thinking about the end of the world.

An hour earlier, I had arrived at the Gare du Nord to find myself the most overdressed man in Paris. It's hot, way too hot for a February morning. I immediately shed my heavy winter coat and, during the hour's walk to this park, my jumper followed. A red admiral butterfly, roused by the unseasonal heat, circles around my bench, as confused as I am by a summer day in the middle of winter. Two bare-chested Parisian men cycle past. Today will later be declared the hottest February day ever recorded in France.

The surrealness of this unseasonal scene is augmented by the bizarre fairground ride that's spinning in front of me. Those hand-painted horses which rise and fall on a traditional carousel have been replaced here by a rotating parade of extinct or near-extinct creatures. Children cling to a green triceratops (extinct 66 million years ago) and a herd of *Sivatherium* (a giraffe-like animal that disappeared one million years ago). There's also an aepyornis, the giant elephant bird of Madagascar (extinct around 1,000 years ago), a dodo (extinct around 350 years ago) and a Tasmanian tiger (extinct 85 years ago). The laughing girl rides on an elephant and there's a panda and gorilla too – representatives of endangered species currently clinging to a perilous existence on a rapidly deteriorating planet as it spins through space. Above the ticket booth a painted dodo casts its judgmental eyes over this cavalcade of extinction while drinking a milkshake through a stripy straw. I'm hypnotised by the juxtaposition of the bright lights, sounds and laughter of this curious carnival against the spectre of death and extinction. I'm so entranced I don't notice my ice cream has melted down my knuckles.

This carousel, the 'Dodo Manège', was opened in 1992 and is one of the more recent attractions in the historic Jardin des Plantes, 10 hectares (28 acres) of park and gardens on the left bank of the Seine. Originally established in 1629 by Louis XIII to grow medicinal herbs, the botanical gardens and associated laboratories and collections would become Europe's leading scientific establishment. In the 1790s, just after the French Revolution, animals were liberated from the private royal menagerie in Versailles, and this public zoo, La Ménagerie, was established here, the second-oldest zoo in the world. Scientists came here to study while Parisians came here to marvel at elephants, lions, giraffes and other exotic creatures. In the 1860s, a most mysterious animal was living here in the Jardin des Plantes: a deer from Siam (or, as it's now known, Thailand).

This deer didn't look particularly strange. It certainly possessed the standard feature you'd hope for in a large male deer: an impressive set of antlers. These antlers were long, frequently forked and they curved and branched in a unique way, which gave them an almost basket-like shape. In 1863, English naturalist Edward Blyth examined a similar pair of antlers given as a gift to Queen Victoria and announced that they must belong to an altogether new species of deer. Blyth named this new animal Schomburgk's deer 'in compliment to his distinguished friend, Her Majesty's representative in the court of Siam' – Sir Robert Schomburgk.

Living specimens of this deer had already been captured by hunters in Siam and exported to European zoos and collections. The stag, which lived here in the Jardin des Plantes, had arrived in 1862, a year before the species was formally identified, and another had previously travelled from Bangkok to the Zoological Gardens in Hamburg in 1860. A particularly wild individual, which arrived in Cologne in 1897, eventually had to be put down because of a 'savage temper that became uncontrollable'. The Schomburgk's deer stag which lived in Berlin Zoological Gardens from 1899 to 1911 was captured on camera, our only known photographs of this species alive.

Yet despite Schomburgk's deer being viewed by thousands of European zoo visitors, there are no records of a European having ever seen one in the wild. The habits and exact whereabouts of the deer remained a mystery. By 1918, it was announced in *The Journal of the Natural History Society of Siam* that Schomburgk's deer was 'on the verge of extinction' and 'It would be a thousand pities if it were to be lost to science before a complete record could be made of it'.

Step forward Brigadier General R. Pigot. I'm not sure I'm entirely convinced by Pigot's scientific intentions. His memoir *Twenty-five Years Big Game Hunting* boasts of bagging brown bears in the Himalayas and tigers in the jungles of India. Nevertheless, in 1928 he travelled through Siam armed with a photograph of Schomburgk's deer and his trusty rifle. Other hunters had sought the deer for its antlers and their alleged healing properties, so Pigot scoured street markets and interrogated Chinese medicine men looking for clues, but drew a blank. It appears that four years earlier Schomburgk's deer antlers had mysteriously stopped appearing in Bangkok's markets. Pigot met one Siamese hunter 'mighty by repute' who recognised the photograph and claimed he knew where to find this deer in the mountains. This tallied with previous reports from mountain tribes such as the Kha Tam Bang ('the men who make themselves invisible'), who claimed to hunt Schomburgk's deer in the high forests with their wooden javelins. Pigot also heard rumours that in Siam's eastern French Territory, Schomburgk's deer were so common that their antlers were used as hat racks. But Pigot was being led on a wild deer chase. All he had discovered was that different species of Siamese deer were known by different names, names which were confusingly interchangeable in different regions. He concluded that, 'while certainly not prepared to say the animal no longer exists, I suspect that it is practically, if not quite, extinct'.

Schomburgk's deer were once found in the great swampy grasslands of central Thailand. Here they would graze in small herds, sometimes in the company of elephants, along the Chao Phraya, the 'River of Kings', which flows for almost 400 kilometres (250 miles) before emptying into the Gulf of Thailand at Bangkok. When the rainy season arrived, the great river's floodplains filled, and deer and other animals were forced on to isolated and exposed islands of grass. It was then that the hunters came. Some paddled dugouts, some rode water buffalo. Some rose from the misty marshes wearing antlers on their heads, disguised as their prey, and stalked the deer with clubs and spears.

Yet the biggest threat to the deer would be economics. From 1855, Siam began signing treaties which allowed trade with other countries. Rice, originally grown just to supply local people, was now grown to supply the world. By the start of the twentieth century, almost all available swamps and grasslands were transformed for cultivation. New railroads brought more and more people deeper into the countryside. Schomburgk's deer retreated into the forests. This deer, so agile, alert and specialised for life on the open swampy plains was trapped among the trees, the stag's proud antlers now a hindrance to movement. Imagine trying to outrun a tiger through the dense forest at night with two hat racks strapped to your head.

The last known wild individuals were shot in September 1932 in forests near the Khwae Noi and Khwae Yai rivers. The final known Schomburgk's deer, a full-grown buck, was apparently kept as a pet in the temple at Maha Chai, 29 kilometres (18 miles) south-west of Bangkok. It wore a small piece of yellow robe and a tiny bell around its neck and was let loose to walk around the temple and local market. One night in 1938 a drunk local man beat it to death with a club. And that was the senseless and brutal end of the majestic Schomburgk's deer.

Hundreds of pairs of Schomburgk's deer antlers remain in museums and collections around the world today, but one particular pair has provided us with a tantalising possibility. In February 1991, a United Nations agronomist photographed a pair of Schomburgk's deer antlers on display in a shop in the province of Phongsali in northern Laos. The antlers appeared to be in a fresh condition.

In research published in 2019, researchers G.B. Schroering and Gary J. Galbreath presented further details of this incredible discovery and made contact with a key witness in the story – the long-distance truck driver who had originally acquired the antlers. The trucker revealed that the antlers were obtained in Khamkeut, hundreds of miles south in central Laos, and confirmed that they were indeed fresh. His claim was supported through analysis of the agronomist's photograph. Among other evidence, the researchers highlighted the condition of the pedicle, the 'stalk' where the antlers had been excised from the skull. 'Even the blood was still reddish', said Galbreath, 'it would have become black with increased age. In the tropics the antlers would not continue to look this way even within a matter of months.'

These bloodied antlers suggested that Schomburgk's deer had survived, possibly as a small relict population, in central or southern Laos until the 1990s, almost 60 years and 805 kilometres (500 miles) away from the last wild sighting. There were other reports of Schomburgk's deer antlers on sale in other markets around the early 1990s too. Had a herd hidden from humans for decades in the hot, humid jungles of Laos, enduring the intensive blanket bombings of the Vietnam War, only to be discovered and wiped out by hunters as the century came to a close?

• • •

Gravel crunches beneath my feet as I navigate the ordered avenues and flowerbeds of the Jardin des Plantes in the February heat and head towards the impressive building that dominates the garden's western edge. Opened to the public in 1889, the Galerie de Zoologie showcased over a million natural history specimens. Shrapnel rained down on the building during the liberation of France in

1944 and, following the Second World War, the museum struggled to maintain the collections and building repairs and closed in 1966. Today, the museum and its exhibits have been renovated, restored and renamed: the Grande Galerie de L'Evolution.

It's not often I get to use the word 'cavernous'; to be fair, I'm not often in a cavern, but there is no other word to describe this huge hall, the hollow heart of the Grande Galerie de L'Evolution. I've taken a glass elevator to the highest of the metal balconies which encircle this vast room. From here a parade of elephants, giraffes and other African mammals is dwarfed far below me. Atmospheric lighting, projections and ambient sound effects recreate a thunderous rainstorm on the 1,000-square-metre (10,700-square-foot) skylight overhead. It takes me 10 minutes to notice the enormous blue whale skeleton tucked away in the corner. After I had succeeded in purchasing my ticket using my limited knowledge of French, I reached the top floor and realised the museum guidebook I was handed was in German, so I now find myself wonderfully confused and lost among the museum's story of evolution. I finally stumble upon the room I've been looking for, almost hidden away adjacent to the museum's main hall: La Salle des Espèces Menacées et des Espèces Disparues (The Hall of Endangered and Extinct Species, or Die Halle der gefährdeten und ausgestorbenen Arten, according to my guidebook).

For months I've been excited about visiting this gallery and I pause momentarily to calm myself before grabbing the ornate brass handle, pushing the heavy door half open and slipping inside. Everything changes. There are no novelty soundscapes or special effects. The only windows, located high on the east wall, are screened by blinds to block the damaging daylight. Instead, the room's light radiates from inside the display cases, where hundreds of specimens are lit with minimal illumination from optical fibre spotlights, leaving most of this long, narrow gallery in shadow. This room dates back to the original Galerie de Zoologie and, with its carved wooden panels and high, vaulted ceiling, there is a chapel-like ambience to this space that demands respect and reverence. Within this silence, every footstep on the polished parquet floor echoes along the gallery.

In the centre of the room, in a freestanding, octagonal glass case, stands the world's only complete specimen of Schomburgk's deer: dignified, elegant, strangely ethereal. In the gallery's gloom, the small, bright spotlights that encircle and illuminate the deer are reflected and multiplied by the internal angles of the glass panels, making the deer glow among a constellation of stars. This is the Schomburgk's deer that arrived in Paris in 1862 and was kept in the Jardin des Plantes until its death in 1868, its body respectfully preserved and mounted. Dying alone in confinement, a world away from its herd on the wide Siamese plains, may seem a tragic end for this stately animal, but it could have been far worse. Two years after its death, during the Prussian siege of the city, desperate Parisians slaughtered the zoo's animals for food. Deer, yaks, camels and kangaroos were consumed first. Even the zoo's beloved elephants, Castor and Pollux, were shot and served. We're lucky this unique specimen of Schomburgk's deer didn't end up in a pie with a zebra. As I circle the deer's display case a family bursts through the gallery's far double doors. Light and laughter flood the room until, confronted by the unnerving aura of the gallery, they freeze as if they have just gatecrashed a funeral. The father hastens them back through the door, leaving me alone again amid the stillness and silence.

I share a few more moments with Schomburgk's deer and then begin to make my way through the room case to case. Flowers, flattened and faded, are pressed against blotting paper pages. Here lies the fragile form of the Cry violet, a French endemic flower, extinct since 1930 through quarrying of its limestone habitat and overzealous botanical collecting. In 2019, botanists announced that 571 plant species were known to have become extinct since 1750, adding that this figure would be an underestimate. This rate of extinction is 500 times what would naturally be expected.

Here are two rare examples of the saddle-backed Rodrigues giant tortoise and the Réunion giant tortoise, both lost around 1800, eaten into extinction along with the two giant tortoise species on the neighbouring island of Mauritius. The world's only surviving skeleton of the Kangaroo Island emu (extinct in 1827 through hunting and the burning of its forests) stands snake-necked in the spotlight. I drift slowly through the silent gallery, pausing to pay my respects at each display case.

Toolache wallaby (extinct around 1939), the Eastern hare wallaby (extinct 1889), the broad-faced potoroo (extinct around 1875).

The gallery's great auk was, unusually, collected in Scotland in 1832 and not from Eldey, the Icelandic island where most specimens were taken and where the last pair were killed in 1844. Our relentless slaughter of this once abundant stately sea bird still appals me, but, looking up, I remember that a century later, in 1944, our bombs rained down on this museum's roof during a war that wiped out 80 million members of our own species. Never underestimate mankind's capacity for mindless destruction.

Carolina parakeet (extinct around 1910), Hawai'i 'ō'ō (extinct 1902), O'ahu 'ō'ō (extinct 1837).

Pinned in a display case among examples of vanished and vanishing butterflies, beetles, wasps and dragonflies are a pair of Xerces blue, perhaps specimens posted back to Paris from the California Gold Rush by Pierre Lorquin himself. In 2019, a report in the journal *Biological Conservation* revealed that 40 per cent of insect species are threatened with extinction in the next few decades. Other recent reports highlight the loss not just of species but insect abundance, warning that this reduction will cause entire terrestrial ecosystems to collapse.

New Zealand quail (extinct around 1870), South Island piopio (extinct around 1900).

And here are my beautiful huia, a pair of course. Seeing them now seems somehow sadder after visiting those silent New Zealand forests which should still echo with their song. I feel deprived of the opportunity to ever see these birds and I recall the deplorable theft of the male huia's tail feathers in 2012 from the small museum in Dannevirke. In July 2020, the museum's huia case would be broken into once more and this time the entire female huia would be snatched and stolen.

Passenger pigeon (extinct 1914), Tasmanian tiger (extinct 1936).

I instantly recognise the unique beaked skull of the magnificent Steller's sea cow. I can't think of this mighty creature without thinking of my hero Georg Steller. I realise why I feel an affinity to Steller. I wouldn't claim to share his intellect, compassion or bravery, but throughout his story I could certainly share his frustration. Steller, trapped aboard the *St Peter*, tried time and time again to use his scientific observations to warn those steering the ship that they were heading towards imminent danger but was ignored until it was too late. These days I feel trapped upon a planet which, scientists warn us, is heading towards an environmental catastrophe, yet those in command, those who could change our course, ignore these warnings and keep their foot on the accelerator.

I'd like to think Steller would have been appreciated here in the Jardin des Plantes. It has been home to some of history's most eminent naturalists: Buffon, Lamarck and Cuvier, the man who lifted the lid on the whole concept of extinction back in 1796. Cuvier didn't stop there. In 1812, he attempted to explain the causes of extinction. He proposed that vanished creatures had been victims of incredible catastrophes or sudden 'revolutions on the surface of Earth', which had wiped 'living organisms without number' from the planet. Cuvier tried to identify what these catastrophes had been. Today, scientists recognise five previous mass extinction events, the last occurring 66 million years ago when an asteroid slammed into Earth, wiping an estimated 75 per cent of species from the planet, destroying the dinosaurs and giving the mammals the big break they had been waiting for.

On 6 May 2019, scientists from the United Nations gathered in Paris to announce the findings of a global study on biodiversity, concluding that 1 million of the world's estimated 8 million species now face extinction, many within decades. Extinction rates vary from tens to hundreds of times higher than they have averaged over the past 10 million years, and that rate is accelerating. The driving forces behind these extinctions are changes in land and sea use, hunting and poaching, climate change, pollution and invasive alien species. Other, more drastic estimates suggest that 40 per cent of the world's species could be lost by 2070. It's 250 years since Cuvier's birth. If he returned today it wouldn't take him too long to figure out where to look to find the next catastrophe that will cause the mass extinction of life on the planet. We're already here.

● ● ●

On my route around the gallery I have avoided one exhibit that seems out of place in this room, but now I turn to confront it. A clock. An extravagant clock designed and built in 1745 for Marie Antoinette, its twitching golden cogs and spinning silver gears a vulgar celebration of greed and arrogance. It stands in stark contrast to the exhibits of true beauty and majesty that stand silent and still in the other display cases, its presence in this room a conceited intrusion.

The time on the clock's ornate dial is the same as that on the broken clock at the Booth Museum, three minutes to twelve. For the extinct species represented in this room the hands of time have been stopped by the hands of man. For other species on display here the clock is still ticking, but their time is running out. Glancing around the gallery at the gorillas, vultures, tigers, albatrosses, orangutans and a hundred others, it's uncomfortably easy to foresee a future where a weary museum curator replaces each 'endangered' label with one which reads 'etiente': extinct. The gallery suddenly feels oppressive, devoid of light, warmth and hope. But maybe that's what the clock's three remaining minutes represent. Hope. The hope that maybe we still have time, time to undo our damage and act to prevent these predicted extinctions. The only certainty is that time will not wait for us.

Tick. Two minutes to twelve. We need to act now. Every one of us must decide whether we are going to be part of the problem or part of the solution. I'm sure Marie Antoinette wouldn't approve of my thinking, but we need a revolution. We need to change.

Tick. One minute to twelve. An accusing voice fills my head asking 'What about you?' In the glass display case I catch sight of my own reflection, a man who has just flown to the other side of the world and back, and I realise I need to change.

Tick. Twelve o'clock. Gears whirr into action. The clock's swinging bells create a cacophony of chimes which reverberates through the gallery, overthrowing the serenity of the entire room. I turn away, searching for some sanctuary – an escape from the commotion. I look again to the animals whose lives I had followed and with whom I had felt an unexpected affinity. But all I see now are bones, feathers and fur, the sad remains of the world's extinct creatures, taxidermy testaments to the havoc we have wreaked upon the world. I need to get out. I retreat towards the far exit, reach for the brass handles and push the door open wide.

• • •

As I step into the next room the midday sun blazes through the grand windows, blinding me. I can just make out a figure stood on a podium in front of me, silhouetted in the sunshine. As my eyes adjust, I recognise the familiar form of another extinct animal, but one which has an entire room dedicated to it. Well, it's the dodo. It's special. This life-size replica is the centrepiece of the museum's dodo exhibition. Illuminated upon the stage, the great bird looks dignified and heroic, the embodiment of everything we have lost and everything we stand to lose. It glares down its long, hooked beak, fixing me with a stern, accusatory stare.

In the midst of this tragedy of extinction the dodo challenges each of us with the ultimate question: 'What part will you play?'

CHAPTER ELEVEN

Ivell's Sea Anemone

Edwardsia ivelli

GONE: 1997

'What did you say your book was about? Extinct creatures?' Mark Carnall, collections manager at Oxford University Museum of Natural History, pushes away from his desk and, rotating in his swivel chair, scans the books and boxes stacked on the shelves of his office. As Mark tells me tales of extinct brine shrimps and Polynesian land snails, my eyes catch sight of something, something which I lost 40 years ago. Sat on Mark's desk, between a book about cephalopods and a stapler, is a microscope slide containing a single filament of white fibre. On an aged, handwritten label is the name of the species that this pale hair belonged to: 'Yeti'. Below in smaller writing are the words 'Kumjung, Nepal' and 'Osman Hill'. Was my long-lost belief in mysterious hairy hominids about to be resurrected?

From 1930, up until his death in 1975, Dr William Osman Hill gained a reputation as one of the world's leading primatologists. He would be the last in a line of distinguished anatomists working at the Zoological Society of London in a position held by Richard Owen over a century before. Yet, during the 1950s, Osman Hill was also fascinated by the possibility that large bipedal primates were lying low in the high Himalayas and amassed a collection of purported pieces of yeti: hair, fur, skin, even a mummified finger. None of these relics would withstand scientific scrutiny as conclusive proof of the existence of the yeti. But they stand as evidence that there was a time, not all that long along ago, when even leading zoologists believed that the world was still big enough to hide monsters. While Mark tells me more about Osman Hill he passes me the slide. I hold it up to the sunlight, squint at the single strand inside and smile, my childhood beliefs somehow vindicated; I had found my yeti. But that wasn't why I had returned to Oxford. I was here in search of something far less abominable.

A few weeks ago, during my joyless Wednesday evening expedition to the local supermarket, I had taken a slight detour. After passing the pylon of cormorants, spread-winged in the setting sun, I turned right, not left, and a few minutes later I was stood at Widewater Lagoon nature reserve. This 1 kilometre (⅔ mile)-long sliver of brackish water, separated from the sea by a shingle ridge, lies landlocked – stranded between a tarmacked car park and an unbroken row of modern homes. I drive by each week but have never had any interest in visiting, until now. I park my car and stand staring over the shallow lagoon. After months researching far-flung locations around the globe, the final resting places of lost species, I had been shocked to discover that Widewater Lagoon, just 10 minutes from my house, was the last known whereabouts of an extinct animal. I study the faded information panel containing illustrated interpretations of the lagoon's wildlife. Among the herons, waders and ducks, a bizarre-looking creature lies sprawled on the mud. Grey and tubular, it resembles a section of somebody's small intestine or maybe a really long sock with wiry tentacles poking out of one end. It is labelled '*Edwardsia ivelli*, Ivell's sea anemone'.

In September 1973, Richard Manuel received an interesting parcel. I like to imagine he tore open the package as excitedly as a child at Christmas – a snowstorm of shredded paper. But while I'd expect a child to be underwhelmed at receiving 20 sea anemones suspended in containers of brackish water, I'm certain Manuel, an expert in British Anthozoa (sea anemones and corals), was over the moon. The specimens had been sent by student Richard Ivell who, while undertaking surveys of Widewater Lagoon as research for his master's thesis, had discovered an unusual anemone that he couldn't identify. Manuel was equally baffled. Some of the anemones were dissected and examined, while the lucky ones were installed in a bowl of sea water and mud for a year, their behaviour observed and recorded. Ivell's unidentified anemones lived their lives burrowed in the soft mud, all that remained visible a crown of 12 translucent tentacles stippled with creamy white and orange dots. Nine of these tentacles lay splayed flat on the sediment's surface while the remaining three were held vertical, sweeping food from the sea water into the creature's mouth. When it sensed danger, the anxious anemone would quickly retract its tentacles, retreating fully into its burrow. In 1975, Manuel would describe these anemones as a species new to science. How Ivell fared with his thesis has been lost to history, but the young student would be forever immortalised as the discoverer of a new animal: *Edwardsia ivelli* – Ivell's sea anemone. But something went wrong. A decade later, Ivell's sea anemone could no longer be located in the lagoon and, after an exhaustive search in 1997, it was declared extinct.

Extinction is not restricted to rainforests and remote islands. It is happening all around you right now. Species are slowly vanishing from our local areas, to be lost in turn from our districts, our counties and our countries. A recent stocktake of Great Britain's wildlife listed 413 animals, plants and fungi which have disappeared from this island in the past 200 years, although almost all of these species still survive – with varying fortunes – elsewhere in

Europe. Ivell's sea anemone was only ever known to exist in one place: Widewater Lagoon. Its disappearance therefore entitled the anemone to membership of an exclusive club – animals once found in Britain that are now globally extinct, a dubious honour it shares with, among others, the great auk, the Irish elk and the woolly mammoth.

• • •

Mark leads me through a maze of low corridors and stairwells down into the basement of the Oxford University Museum of Natural History. He unlocks a door and we enter the spirit store. Some brand-new shelving units are lined with hundreds of modern airtight storage jars, each containing a pickled specimen of something ancient and slightly sinister. It's how I imagine Dr Frankenstein's laboratory would look if he shopped at Ikea. The adjacent room has yet to receive an upgrade, and the shelves are sparsely stacked with a variety of jars of all shapes and sizes containing specimens in clear or yellowing solutions. Mark places a tall, narrow jar with a domed glass stopper on the chemical stained tabletop. I put on my glasses to read its handwritten label: '*Edwardsia ivelli*', '4 Sept 1973', 'Widewater Lagoon', '½ to 1 metre depth'. Inside are two glass tubes containing a solution of 75 per cent ethanol and floating in the ethanol . . . nothing. 'I can assure you they are in there', Mark promises me and leans in to join the search. 'There, at the bottom.' I raise the jar up to the storeroom's light bulb and only then can I make out a thin squiggle, hardly bigger than a yeti's hair, suspended in the tubes. 'Is that *it*?' There's no disguising my disappointment.

I thought sea anemones were those chunky, strawberry-sized blobs whose tentacles would grip my tiny fingers when, as a child, I'd antagonised them in a rock pool. But this? I had harboured a hope that, after failing to find the South Island kōkako, maybe I could be the man to rediscover Ivell's sea anemone in Widewater Lagoon. The fact that I couldn't rediscover it in a small tube a couple of inches from my face didn't inspire me with confidence.

● ● ●

A week later and it's three minutes to twelve again. I'm back at the Booth Museum of Natural History and I pause once more in front of its cabinet of extinct creatures. I had stood right here a year ago, at a time in my life when things felt particularly hopeless. This motley assortment of vanished animals had reminded me of a childhood filled with fascination, wonder and endless possibilities. They had inspired a journey in search of something now missing from my life, something that was gone. If I was looking for hope then this ragged band were an unlikely team to fill me with optimism; stories of extinction tend to be short on happy endings – yet the search itself had sustained and lifted me.

I lean in, eye to eye, with the 'Grey Ghost', the South Island kōkako, still perched, resolutely, on the shelf of extinction. I truly wish I could share the belief that this bird was still alive out there, somewhere hidden behind New Zealand's rugged ranges. Because a belief in the South Island kōkako is a belief that mankind has not completely wrecked this planet, that the Earth is still big enough to withstand us. But I had found hope elsewhere during my journey. In New Zealand I had encountered the takahē, the preposterous purple bird which had resurfaced after 50 years missing in action. The antlers of Schomburgk's deer glimpsed in a Laos shop in 1991 and the tantalising tortoise discovered on Fernandina Island in 2019 gave optimism for the survival of these species way beyond their accepted expiry dates. Elsewhere during 2019 and 2020, the Vietnamese mouse-deer, the Somali elephant shrew and the starry night harlequin toad of Colombia – all previously feared to be extinct – had returned to the land of the living. And throughout my travels I had visited some of the world's most incredible museums and witnessed the vital and increasingly crucial work they are undertaking in educating, inspiring and motivating people to take action to save our planet. In the face of the biodiversity crisis, that dark night that looms ahead of us, I had found just enough faith to believe that things can change.

The Booth Museum's extinction display is due to be dismantled soon. It's being removed to make way for a new exhibition, and the specimens will be separated and returned to storage, taking their stories with them. There was a movie I saw once. All I remember about it was Al Pacino and one line of dialogue, something about how we die twice, once when the breath leaves our body, and once when the last person says our name. I hope that, through telling the stories of these extinct creatures, I've done my bit to help keep them alive a little longer.

I've started volunteering at the museum, assisting with cataloguing their collections and helping with their public events, which raise awareness of local and global conservation issues. Sat in the back office one afternoon, I chatted with the museum staff about my interest in our local extinction icon, Ivell's sea anemone, and it was suggested that I should speak to Dr Gerald Legg. Gerald has recently retired as the Booth Museum's keeper of natural sciences, but his fascination with the natural world is irrepressible. He's been undertaking subaqua surveys of marine life for many years and, when I meet with him at the Booth, he agrees to join me on an intrepid expedition to the lagoon down the road from my house. Our target is just 1.5 centimetres (⅔ inch) long, although that bit is buried in the mud. All we'd ever hope to see are the anemone's 6-millimetre (¼-inch) see-through tentacles which it will withdraw in a flash if it senses us approaching. This isn't going to be easy, but Gerald has a suggestion. Some species of sea anemone fluoresce under ultraviolet light. Floating out across the lagoon at night while shining UV light on to the mud below might make the anemone's tentacles glow like a tiny neon medusa. It's a slim chance, but it may be the best one we have of finding Ivell's sea anemone. I like Gerald's idea and optimism, and I already have a UV torch, a cheap eBay purchase that I have never used. All I need now is something to float on.

'It's a crocodile.' 'Yes. I know. Do you have something against crocodiles?' My friend has offered to lend me an inflatable mattress so I can assist in tonight's survey and I've swung by her house on my way to the lagoon. What she had neglected to mention was that the inflatable was shaped like a smiling six-foot crocodile. She has already pumped it up for me especially, so, not wanting to seem ungrateful, I thank her and wrestle it into the car.

I arrive at the lagoon 10 minutes early and watch a cormorant fishing in the dying light as the summer sun sets behind the chalets. Staring out across the water, I wonder what had happened to Ivell's sea anemone. Widewater had been its entire world. Saline lagoons such as this one are fragile habitats vulnerable to fluctuating salinity and temperature, desiccation and pollution. We can only assume that, at some point, some crucial element of the anemone's environment changed to such an extent that it could no longer survive in the only place it was known to exist. Our planet is the only place that we know of where life exists. And now our environment is changing, rapidly driving a million species towards extinction and threatening our future. I think about the tiny, transparent sea anemone that once lived here. It was powerless to prevent its world from changing. But we are not.

• • •

The cheery beep of a car horn startles me and I turn to see Gerald arriving. He's come prepared and he pulls on his neoprene wetsuit, inflates a rigid paddleboard and adjusts the settings on an expensive water-resistant UV lamp. I decide not to mention my cheap torch or the inflatable crocodile on the back seat of my car. Ten minutes later Gerald is gliding across the lagoon, flat on his paddleboard, his face inches from the water's surface. He methodically sweeps his UV lamp in the water, illuminating the lagoon bed ahead of him in a shimmering halo of blue light.

I tentatively wade into the water. I switch on my UV torch, which blinks half-heartedly; its weak, flickering blue beam throws light on a shoal of tiny, silver fish and an irate crab, which scuttles towards me, waving a claw as if warning me to turn back. I should have taken its advice. A few feet from the shore, I sink halfway up to my knees in the sludgy black mud. It's deeper than I imagined and, as I retrieve my foot, I stir up clouds of billowing black sediment. I stare blindly into the gloop and the gloom, completely dispirited. This is pointless; I'm wasting my time. I'm about to give up when Gerald, who seems to have mastered his search technique, raises his head and calls across from the far shore, 'You won't see anything if you wade through it, you have to float.'

And so, here's where I'll end my story for now. Drifting across a lagoon on an inflatable crocodile, my nose skimming the water. I'm trying not to swallow a mouthful of saltwater or fog my vision by stirring up too much sediment. I'm out here floating over the black, murky clouds with a faulty torch, searching for something shining in the darkness. I guess that's what hope is after all.

Stories of Extinction Map

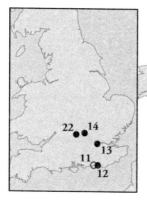

*United King
(see*

*Pacific
Ocean*

*Atlantic
Ocean*

Species Locations ○
1 Eldey (Great Auk)
2 Bering Island (Spectacled Cormorant)
3 Bering Island (Steller's Sea Cow)
4 Otago (Upland Moa)
5 Tararua Ranges (Huia)
6 Heaphy Track (South Island Kōkako)
7 San Francisco (Xerces Blue)
8 Pinta Island (Pinta Island Giant Tortoise)
9 Mauritius (Dodo)
10 Central Thailand (Schomburgk's Deer)
11 Widewater Lagoon (Ivell's Sea Anemone)

Museums ●
12 The Booth Museum of Natural History
13 The Natural History Museum
14 The Natural History Museum at Tring
15 The Natural History Museum of Denmark
16 LUOMUS Finnish Museum of Natural History
17 Otago Museum
18 Museum of New Zealand Te Papa Tongarewa
19 Dannevirke Gallery of History
20 California Academy of Sciences
21 American Museum of Natural History
22 Oxford University Museum of Natural History
23 Grande Galerie de l'Évolution

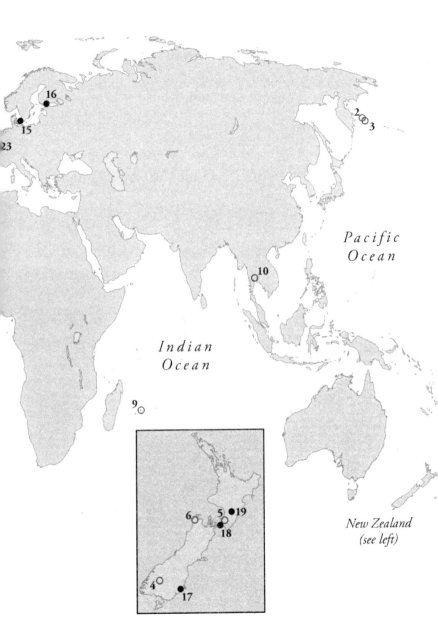

*Pacific
Ocean*

*Indian
Ocean*

*New Zealand
(see left)*

Museums

There are thousands of natural history museums around the world. Through curating our history they are inspiring a better future for our planet. Visit a natural history museum near you and start your own journey of discovery. These are the museums that feature in this book.

The Booth Museum of Natural History, Brighton

brightonmuseums.org.uk/booth

Edward Booth's gift to the people of Brighton is now one of Britain's best-loved natural history museums. Wander among Booth's pioneering dioramas in this temple to taxidermy. You'll also find a merman, the 'Toad in the Hole' (a mummified toad) and modern galleries dedicated to evolution and conservation.

The Natural History Museum of Denmark, Copenhagen

snm.ku.dk

Home to the last great auk organs, the 'other' dodo skull and a gallery of 'precious things' including Hans Christian Andersen's snails, Charles Darwin's barnacles, Misty the Diplodocus and Denmark's loneliest spider. There's also a superb interactive evolution exhibition.

The Natural History Museum at Tring

www.nhm.ac.uk/visit/tring

The wonderful Victorian museum that belongs in a museum. Step back in time and explore Walter Rothschild's incredible collection, including his beloved tortoises, and learn more about 'the man, the museum and the menagerie'.

LUOMUS Finnish Museum of Natural History, Helsinki

www.luomus.fi/en

The collections held by LUOMUS consist of over 13 million specimens and samples, making up over 50 per cent of all natural history collections in Finland. On display amongst the splendid 'Story of Bones' exhibition you'll find the world's most complete Steller's sea cow skeleton.

Otago Museum, Dunedin

otagomuseum.nz

Beautifully curated collections represent the cultural and natural history of New Zealand's Otago region. There are fantastic displays of moa and other extinct bird species. Look out for their rare specimen of the Falkland Islands wolf (extinct 1876). Don't forget to donate a dollar to the talking moa when you leave.

The Natural History Museum, London

www.nhm.ac.uk

The 'cathedral to nature' and the highlight of any visit to London. You'll find Richard Owen's moa bone fragment, Mary Anning's ichthyosaur, Dippy the Diplodocus, a great auk, a Mantellisaurus and a thousand more national treasures.

Dannevirke Gallery of History

14 Gordon Street, Dannevirke, New Zealand

This marvellous rural museum, lovingly maintained and run by local volunteers, tells the history of the small town of Dannevirke on the North Island. You'll find stories of the area's Māori heritage, its Scandinavian settlers and the High Street's Great Fire of 1917.

Museum of New Zealand Te Papa Tongarewa

www.tepapa.govt.nz

The museum's Māori name, 'Te Papa Tongarewa', means 'our container of treasured things and people that spring from mother earth here in New Zealand'. This modern museum contains inspiring galleries of New Zealand history, natural history and Māori culture. My favourite exhibit is that icon of modern bird conservation: the kākāpō ejaculation helmet.

California Academy of Sciences, San Francisco

www.calacademy.org

It feels like the entire planet is here under the Academy's (green) roof. Discover a butterfly-filled rainforest, the African plains, penguins, a coral reef, a planetarium, collections holding 46 million specimens and many interactive 'hands on' exhibits. There's also a massive albino alligator called Claude (which you can't put your hands on).

American Museum of Natural History, New York

www.amnh.org

Escape the New York streets and lose yourself in a world of stunning dioramas showcasing wildlife scenes from all over the planet. Wander amongst mastodons, meteorites and minerals and marvel at the wonders held in the extensive dinosaur exhibition halls.

Oxford University Museum of Natural History, Oxford

www.oumnh.ox.ac.uk

The spectacular neo-Gothic architecture alone would be reason enough to visit this museum. Below the magnificent glass and iron roof and the ornate columns, capitals and corbels you'll find a wonderland of fascinating exhibits including dodos, plesiosaurs and the bones of the 'Red Lady' of Paviland.

Grande Galerie de l'Évolution, Paris

www.jardindesplantesdeparis.fr/en
Forget the Louvre, the real works of art are on display here in this cavernous museum in the Jardin des Plantes. Be amazed by the splendour and diversity of nature before stepping into La Salle des Espèces Menacées et des Espèces Disparues (The Room of Endangered and Extinct Species) and experiencing its sad beauty.

Charities

There will be nature conservation organisations local to you, in your community, county and country, that would appreciate your support to help them to protect wildlife. Join one today. The following charities are particularly relevant to the species and issues discussed in this book.

BirdLife International
www.birdlife.org
The world leader in bird conservation, undertaking rigorous science and projects in important sites and habitats for the conservation of birds and all nature.

Forest and Bird
www.forestandbird.org.nz
New Zealand's leading independent conservation organisation, bringing positive change to New Zealand's land, fresh water, oceans and climate.

Galápagos Conservancy
www.galapagos.org
Protecting the unique biodiversity and ecosystems of the Galápagos Islands by supporting research and management, informing public policy, and building a sustainable society.

Global Wildlife Conservation
www.globalwildlife.org
Collaborating directly with partners worldwide to protect wildlife and their habitats. Focused on often overlooked but

highly threatened species and ecosystems integral to the health of our planet.

The South Island Kōkako Charitable Trust

www.southislandkokako.org
Dedicated to planning and coordinating research to bring about the discovery and recovery of New Zealand's 'Grey Ghost'.

The Wildlife Trusts

www.wildlifetrusts.org
A federation of 46 independent wildlife conservation charities covering the whole of the UK. Each Wildlife Trust is an independent charity formed by people getting together to make a positive difference to wildlife and future generations.

World Land Trust

www.worldlandtrust.org
Working with partners and communities throughout the world to provide permanent protection to the world's most biologically significant and threatened habitats, acre by acre.

The Xerces Society

www.xerces.org
The Xerces blue butterfly is immortalised through the work of this science-based, non-profit organisation that protects wildlife through the conservation of invertebrates and their habitats.

Further Reading

John Burton (1975) *The How and Why Wonder Book of Extinct Animals* (Transworld)

Errol Fuller (1987) *Extinct Birds* (Viking Rainbird)

Errol Fuller (1999) *The Great Auk* (Errol Fuller)

Errol Fuller (2002) *Dodo: From Extinction to Icon* (Harper Collins)

Ross Galbreath (1989) *Walter Buller: The Reluctant Conservationist* (GP Books)

Jeremy Gaskell (2000) *Who Killed The Great Auk?* (OUP Oxford)

George Gibbs (2016) *Ghosts of Gondwana* (Potton & Burton)

Julian Hume (2017) *Extinct Birds* (Bloomsbury Natural History)

Matthew James (2017) *Collecting Evolution: The Galapagos Expedition that Vindicated Darwin* (OUP USA)

Boonsong Lekagul & Jeffrey McNeely (1978) *Mammals of Thailand* (Association for the Conservation of Wildlife)

Colin Miskelly (ed.) *New Zealand Birds Online.* www.nzbirdsonline.org.nz

Geoff Norman (2018) *Birdstories: A History of the Birds of New Zealand* (Potton & Burton)

Jane Pickering (2010) *The Oxford Dodo: The Sad Story of the Ungainly Bird That Became an Oxford Icon* (Oxford University Museum of Natural History)

Miriam Rothschild (2008) *Walter Rothschild: The Man, the Museum and the Menagerie* (Natural History Museum)

Robert Silverberg (1973) *The Dodo, The Auk and the Oryx* (Puffin)

Georg Wilhelm Steller (1751) *De Bestiis Marinis, or, The Beasts of the Sea*

Georg Wilhelm Steller, ed. O.W. Frost (1988) *Journal of a Voyage with Bering, 1741–1742* (Stanford)

Richard Wolfe (2003) *Moa. The Dramatic Story of the Discovery of a Giant Bird* (Penguin)

Index

Acknowledgements

Thank you to the following people (and reptiles) for their inspiration, assistance and for putting me up / putting up with me on my travels: Clare Blencowe, Lois Mayhew, Laurie Jackson, Mark Greco, Helen Burgess, Lou Atkins, Olivia O'Driscoll, Roger & Sarah Frost, Sean Clancy, Tim Parmenter, Tootles.

This book would not have happened without Monica Perdoni (Leaping Hare Press) bombarding me with banana bread and encouragement until I agreed to write it. Thanks also to my patient editor Laura Bulbeck and the team at Quarto. Thank you to Jade They for bringing these animals to life with her wonderful illustrations.

I am indebted to the museum staff, scientists and naturalists from all over the world who kindly shared their knowledge, research and time: Grace Brindle, John Cooper, Kerrie Curzon, Lee Ismail and Sarah Wilson (The Booth Museum of Natural History), Jessica Bevan née Thomas (Swansea University), Peter A. Hosner (Natural History Museum of Denmark), Mark Adams (Natural History Museum, Tring), Junya Watanabe (University of Cambridge), Alexander Aleixo and Martti Hildén (LUOMUS Finnish Museum of Natural History), Kane Fleury (Otago Museum), Bill Jackson (Honeycomb Hill Cave), Charmaine Petereit (Ngarua Caves), Derry Kingston (Heaphy Track), Nancy Wadsworth (Dannevirke Gallery of History), Colin Miskelly (Museum of New Zealand Te Papa Tongarewa), David Bettman, Chris Grinter, Lauren A. Scheinberg (California Academy of Sciences), Sandra

Chapman, Chris Raper and Florin Feneru (Natural History Museum, London), Ryan Mitchell, Mark Carnall, Eileen Westwig (Oxford University Museum of Natural History), Gary Galbreath (Northwestern University), Nikki McArthur, George and Keena Gibbs, Liam O'Brien, Gerald Legg, Ralfe and Clare Whistler.